VUCA Masters:

Developing Leadership Agility Fitness for the New World of Work

Nicholas F. Horney, Ph.D.

an imprint of

BAI press sntio. press

No big change is successful unless it starts with the leaders. This book, by an outstanding Vuca Master, is a practical guide for developing your leadership agility fitness full of inspiring real world examples.

Yesim Pinar Kitapci
CEO at Koç Finansman A.Ş.
Member of the board at
Association of Financial Institutions
Recognized as one of the most powerful
women leaders in Turkey by the Ekonomist

Our world is getting increasingly more complex every day. Information is always updating and leaders need to adapt quickly as conditions change. The recent global pandemic has affected everyone of us and businesses have had to think differently in order to survive. The VUCA Masters: Developing Leadership Agility Fitness for the New World of Work provides key guidance for navigating through these new obstacles. The leaders of tomorrow will learn the principles of agility and be able to pivot their organization to remain relevant and competitive. Our industry and our customers depend on it. I highly recommend VUCA Masters as an essential leadership development resource for all of my colleagues in Women in Nuclear to assess and develop their leadership agility fitness.

Carol Barajas
VP Steam Generator Replacement
Tennessee Valley Authority (TVA)

As a practicing neurologist, I find Nick's proposition in the book to provide welcome clarity for leadership agility development in healthcare: just as one strives for physical fitness and should seek routine evaluations of that fitness, so must leaders invest in true "agility fitness;" and regularly checking on agility "vital signs" is a must. Leaders who achieve a high level of agility fitness Nick calls "VUCA Masters." His book, which includes a separate practitioner's guide, provides a very practical approach for leaders in all fields to follow for their development. I am looking forward to sharing his book with my colleagues in the healthcare industry so that they can work with a coach to conduct an annual Leadership Agility Fitness exam and create their development plan to better enable them to deal with future VUCA events in our New World of Work.

Dr. Keith Willis
Neurologist and Medical Group Leader

To call Dr. Horney a leader ahead of his time is really an understatement. He understood the crucial need for agility long before others were beginning to even consider the concept.

I'm delighted that his book and companion practitioner's guide are now available for leaders everywhere. I've personally benefitted from Dr. Horney's coaching, and his practical strategies and solutions have transformed my own leadership approach.

This book is the guide that all leaders need as we work to recover from the challenges of the past year. We all need agility in this volatile, uncertain, complex, and ambiguous environment. Dr. Horney teaches how to achieve that agility.

I found additional value in the VUCA Master Profiles where the profiles of leaders I've long admired (and some new additions) really help to show the real-world applications of agile leadership.

The VUCA Masters is now at the top of my essential leadership resources, and is something I will return to regularly to keep my leadership skills and approach relevant and effective.

Dimitri Benak
Vice President, People & Culture
LoyaltyOne

I have seldom experienced a more well-timed book than "VUCA Masters - Developing Leadership Agility Fitness for the New World of Work". The need for Leadership Agility could not be greater than right now, in the wake of the diminishing pandemic. What I like in particular about the book is the metaphor for health and fitness for Leadership. Also, the book gives loads of practical, easy-to-use examples for the changing workplace and how to lead in turbulent times. A must-read for any leader or HR professional who would like to adapt their leadership skills to the next level, post-Corona.

Pia-Maria Thorén
Inspiration Director and Agile People Coach
co-author of #agilepeoplemanifesto
Agile People AB

ISBN 978-1-957600-06-2 (paperback)
ISBN 978-1-957600-07-9 (ebook)

*Design — Danilo S (cover, typesetting, book),
Marina M (Illustrations)
Editorial — BAI Editorial Board*

First Edition 2021.

BAI press
an imprint of sntioPress

sntioPress,
a publishing venture of Sntio, LLC
511 Ave of the Americas, #4047,
New York, NY 10011

telephone
+1 (917) 740-2269
+44 7480 790020

email
press@sntio.net

web
www.sntiopress.com
businesssagility.institute

Citations of Agility Consulting Intellectual Property reflects the work of
Dr. Nick Horney and Tom O'Shea.

Chapters

FOREWORD: VUCA MASTERS

VUCA: Volatility, Uncertainty, Complexity, Ambiguity. By the late 1980's it was a perfect description of the global security scene. And our armed forces were struggling to understand what it all meant: the Warsaw Pact and the Soviet Union were clearly in trouble, and by the end of 1989, the Berlin Wall had fallen; less than two years later, the Soviet Union itself disappeared. Suddenly, what had been an organizing principle for the US Army for generations – fighting and winning a high-intensity war on the plains of northern Europe -- had vanished. In the meantime, nearly simultaneously, reports of Yugoslavia's potential dissolution began to fill the pages of our intelligence reports, along with fears of ethnic and religious divisions in a region known for violently settling old scores.

Throughout much of the period just described, I was the Director of Strategy, Plans, and Policy for the US Army. These were heady days for strategists. Each of us in the "strategy community" was focused on trying to understand what these historic changes meant for our armed forces in a post-Cold War world. In my talks to military audiences during this period, I used the opening lines of an old song by the Buffalo Springfield to set the stage for what those of us in uniform were facing: "There's something's happenin' here, what it is ain't exactly clear." My focus was on what this new environment suggested for how our Army might organize, train, and equip itself in the years ahead; I did not address what these changes meant for leadership, particularly for senior Army leaders.

Fortunately, the Army War College, the service's senior school in the Army's professional military education system, stepped forward in the early 90's to address how leaders should view the new strategic environment. The acronym the War College used as a descriptor of this environment? VUCA. It turned out that the War College's timing was perfect: as the 90's progressed, Yugoslavia disintegrated and the Balkans were aflame; Somali war lords thwarted well-intentioned humanitarian efforts; and global terrorism raised its ugly head. These challenges, and many others, further defined the "VUCA environment" for America's Army and Armed Forces.

Nicholas F. Horney, Ph.D.   9

By the end of the 90's, it was becoming increasingly clear that VUCA had far wider applicability than as a descriptor of challenges facing senior leaders in uniform. Scholars and leadership practitioners like Nick Horney took the VUCA model and projected it "from battlefield to boardroom." Globalization and technological change, by the turn of the century, had transformed the business environment as dramatically as the end of the Cold War had transformed the national security environment.

Horney's own experiences in the Navy's special operations community reinforced his view that the best prescription for leaders at all levels to navigate and succeed in a VUCA environment was to internalize and demonstrate leadership agility. Indeed, my own experiences later in the decade reflected a similar approach: for five years, from 1996 to 2001, I served as the Superintendent of the US Military Academy at West Point. My Dean during most of this period was Brigadier Fletcher Lamkin, and he had refined a lecture to his faculty and the West Point cadets entitled "Leading in a Complex and Uncertain World." Neither General Lamkin nor I used the "VUCA" term, but the environment we described was identical to what the War College had spelled out in the late 80's, and what Nick Horney was describing a decade later. And the West Point Dean and Superintendent's strong advice to the cadets who were to be commissioned as young officer leaders? Develop and practice leadership agility!

Nick Horney has been for years a recognized national and international expert on leadership, organizational behavior, and change management. Few authors or organizational behavior specialists world-wide have had as much impact on instilling the importance of Leadership Agility. Indeed, the consulting firm which Nick founded, "Agility Consulting and Training," received a rare US Patent Office "Mark" in 2002 for the AGILE model; and that model is the foundation for Nick's latest book, VUCA Masters: Developing Leadership Agility Fitness for the New World of Work.

Nick's proposition in the book is straight forward: just as one strives for physical fitness and should seek routine evaluations of that fitness, so must leaders invest in true "agility fitness;" and regularly checking on agility "vital signs" is a must. Leaders who achieve a high level of agility fitness Nick calls "VUCA Masters." His book, which includes a separate practitioner's guide, readably lays out how that master's level is achieved.

For anyone with a recent Army background, the concept of "Master Fitness" resonates. Physical Fitness badges are coveted, and Master Fitness Trainer Courses remain popular. Because the Army is a physically demanding profession, "fitness" has been a core evaluation metric for soldiers and leaders for generations. One of the many attractions of Horney's VUCA Masters is the "fitness" metaphor he uses to underscore what "Leadership Agility Fitness" means in the 21st century workplace; agility fitness will quickly become a core attribute for success for the next generation of leaders -- in every profession!

The Army War College may have introduced "VUCA." And other authors and institutions have certainly stressed "leadership agility." But Nick Horney has refined, popularized, and operationalized what the two together mean for leadership development. Generations of leaders have benefited from the insights Nick and his team at Agility Consulting have introduced to the leadership literature and debate. Going forward, as the rate of change in our operating environments across the board continues to accelerate, understanding how to develop Leadership Agility -- and more importantly, how to assess and improve your "Agility Fitness" – will be THE essential task for leaders at all levels. VUCA Masters will prove to be indispensable guide for leadership development in the "New World of Work." Especially as the globe slowly recovers from COVID and rethinks the nature of work itself, Dr. Nick Horney has given us all a vitally important and timely read.

Daniel W. Christman
Lieutenant General (retired), USA
55th Superintendent, US Military Academy

Nicholas F. Horney, Ph.D.   11

Introduction - VUCA Masters

Annual Physical Exam -- As I plan for my next physical, I think about the results of my last physical exam and the associated plan of action discussed with my doctor. My individualized plan included regular exercise, healthy and balanced dietary habits, sleep at least 7 hours each night and daily intake of prescribed meds for slightly elevated blood pressure. So when I show up at the doctor's office, the nurse guides me immediately to the scales for my weight. As I look at the results on the scale, it looks like I will need to adjust my plan and focus more on my dietary habits since I'm exercising regular-ly, taking my meds and sleeping between 6-7 hours each night. Fortunately, my blood work looks pretty good and fits within the normal range for my age and sex. My doc-tor asks me some questions about my fitness plan, checks my vital signs and thumps and prods as doctors typical-ly do. He discusses the results of my physical and helps identify any modifications/adjustments needed for my fitness plan. Although this is very simplified illustration, does this annual physical process sound familiar to you?

Annual Leadership Agility Fitness Exam -- Do you have a similar process for checking your "leadership agility vital signs" to help you adjust and adapt to the VUCA you may be experiencing in your business environment?

A McKinsey health survey in 2021 reported that approximately 50% of wellness spending is on products and services that promote better health. My guess is that Leadership Agility Fitness spending is less than 5% of overall spending on agility-related or leadership development investments. How do you think an organization's business agility would benefit if its leaders annually invested in their individual leadership agility fitness development the same way they invested in their annual health (fitness) exams?

Whether you are reading a business book, article or whitepaper or viewing a You-Tube video about organizational transformation, the same story repeats over and over regardless of the organizational discipline -- **if want your organization to change, top leadership must be committed to the change.** Survey research from multiple sources reinforce the notion about the critical importance of leadership's commitment in order to ensure change will occur. A recent research report from the Business Agility Institute (BAI, 2021 Business Agility Study) echoed the importance of leadership commitment for Business Agility Transformation to be successful. But a single change or organizational pivot is not enough to ensure that your organization is ready for the New World of Work, which was dramatically demonstrated during the COVID-19 Pandemic. Therefore, the primary purpose of this book is to help you understand and apply the Leadership Agility Fitness mindset and behavior demanded by a VUCA business environment to identify the need, initiate action and sustain change in a variety of situations, no matter whether the change is perceived to be large or small.

My book and its companion practitioner guide will help you as a leader understand the business imperative of becoming a VUCA Master (defined by a high level of Leadership Agility Fitness) and investing in the development of others to become VUCA Masters. While the fundamental purpose of the book is to provide the background, context and relevance of becoming a VUCA Master, the practitioner guide will provide a roadmap for becoming a VUCA Master and coaching/mentoring others on their VUCA Master journey.

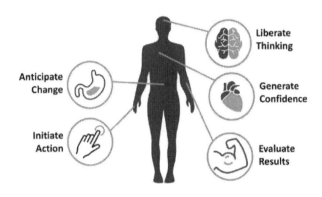

Throughout the book, I will use a physical fitness metaphor to help provide a new way of viewing Leadership Agility. In other words, regardless of age or sex, we can all relate to the value of an annual physical to help understand how well we are doing with our fitness plan, if we have one. At a minimum, my annual physical, which typically includes bloodwork, with my doctor ("coach"), will provide me with data that can help focus my fitness plan until my next physical. Now ask yourself, how you are doing on your annual Leadership Agility Fitness plan.... the same question you might ask about your annual physical fitness? Do you know if you have made any progress on last year's plan? How might you need to modify your Leadership Agility Fitness plan based on your progress, business environmental turbulence, etc.? Perhaps the worst case scenario is that you have no plan at all and can't answer the previous questions. What would you do (or what would your doctor say) if you had no plan of action based on your annual physical? Do you just wait until your lack of personal fitness requires you to be rushed to the hospital's emergency room? As an organizational leader, your Leadership Agility Fitness has implications for others in your organization as well as you and the "emergency room" might be the loss of jobs of those working with you as well as yours.

VUCA Masters will help you create or reinforce the leadership agility fitness mindset which will energize your Leadership Agility Fitness behavior and annual planning (or more frequently, as needed) with the same focus you have on your yearly business plan. As in the case of your annual physical where you meet with your physician, you might find value in meeting with an experienced Leadership Coach to help provide the relevant data and coaching needed to adjust and adapt your individualized Leadership Agility Fitness Plan.

Most doctors and fitness experts will agree that peak physical fitness is a combination of at least the five contributors that I have provided in this illustration below. Muscle building or aerobic exercise alone or even combined will not enable a person to be in peak physical condition. It requires a combination of at least the five illustrated here to enable you to achieve peak physical fitness.

1. Muscle Building Exercise (strength)
2. Aerobic Exercise (run, bike, walk)
3. Flexibility Exercise (stretching)
4. Sleep – About 8 Hours (unaided)
5. Meals – Balanced Nutrition

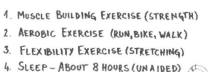

We all know that no one measure (e.g. weight, heart-rate, cholesterol level, blood pressure, etc.) from a physical exam will provide you a comprehensive view of your physical fitness. It takes multiple tests that are interpreted with the aid of a trained physician and perhaps personal trainer to help you create your fitness plan.

Since I began my research and consulting on the topic of Leadership Agility in 2001, I have evolved my thinking to a new way of describing Leadership Agility. Let me use physical fitness to illustrate this new concept of Leadership Agility Fitness™. Fitness is defined as the quality or state of being fit and healthy. The modern definition of fitness describes either a person's ability to perform a specific function or a holistic definition of human adaptability to cope with various situations. Regarding specific function, fitness is attributed to persons who possess significant aerobic or anaerobic ability, i.e. endurance or strength. A well-rounded fitness program improves a person in all aspects of fitness compared to focusing only on one, such as only cardio/respiratory endurance or only weight training.

Global leadership research combined with leadership case studies and reinforced by the Covid-19 Pandemic have concluded that one of the primary characteristics of great leaders is Leadership Agility. A useful definition of Leadership Agility is the ability of a leader to dynamically sense and respond to changes in the environment with actions that are focused, fast and flexible (Horney & O'Shea, 2015). Leadership Agility Fitness is a core capability required for leadership success whether working as a project team leader, functional department head, C-suite executive or serving as a leadership coach at any level. I will refer to leaders who demonstrate exceptional leadership agility fitness as VUCA Masters.

LEADERSHIP AGILITY FITNESS™ -- 5 MAJOR CONTRIBUTORS

1. ANTICIPATE CHANGE
2. GENERATE CONFIDENCE
3. INITIATE ACTION
4. LIBERATE THINKING
5. EVALUATE RESULTS

The Agile Model®

Leadership Agility Fitness is not another change management methodology nor an agile software technique, such as SCRUM. It does represent a new way to focus on the fitness of leaders in a world that is defined by volatility, uncertainty, complexity and ambiguity (VUCA). Just as health is much more than absence of disease, total fitness extends beyond the mere absence of physical, mental, or spiritual injury to include factors such as physical well-being, diet, spirituality, friendships, acclimation to environment, etc. – all factors that promote optimal performance. As with the concept of total fitness, Leadership Agility Fitness is more than flexibility or speed, but a combination of factors. It is also more than resilience or change management since it also requires the capability of anticipatory or preemptive action.

Companies as well as entire industries are wrestling with remaining relevant to consumers in an age of transformational change (e.g., publishing, healthcare, telecommunications, retail, etc.). How can we decode the critical ingredients of leadership agility and define the leadership behavior combinations which result in ultra-fit leadership agility? What examples are there of leaders who have illustrated various Levels and Types of Leadership Agility? Why are these questions relevant or important to us now and in the future?

Nicholas F. Horney, Ph.D.   21

Leadership Agility Fitness is a framework that encourages true balance of the 5 key drivers found in The AGILE Model® (Agility Consulting, 2002), with respect to a rapidly changing VUCA environment. The amount, volume, velocity, intensity, etc. of "noise" we encounter with change requires us to become more agile. And the secret to becoming more agile as a Leader is to demonstrate that you can be focused, fast and flexible, even in the worst circumstances. The AGILE Model® offers the framework that will enable you to identify your Leadership Agility Fitness Level (AFL) and help identify a plan to help you attain and sustain the highest leadership agility fitness level you are willing to achieve.

But it takes work, just like it takes work to achieve your personal physical fitness goal. When effectively integrated into daily leadership behavior, this plan for leadership agility fitness provides the most effective strategy for leaders to survive and thrive in a very turbulent world today and into the future.

In our experience, leadership agility fitness demands competence in a number of specific capabilities as outlined in The Agile Model®:

1. Anticipate Change: Interpret the potential impact of business turbulence and trends along with the implications to the enterprise.

2. Generate Confidence: Create a culture of confidence and engagement of all associates into effective and collaborative teams.

3. Initiate Action: Provide the fuel and the systems to make things happen proactively and responsively ... at all levels of the organization.

4. Liberate Thinking: Create the climate and conditions for fresh solutions by empowering, encouraging and teaching others to be innovative.

5. Evaluate Results: Keeping the focus and managing the knowledge to learn and improve from actions.

Those specific capabilities stem from multiple disciplines of academic research, best practices from numerous organizations and industries, and our practical experience in determining what matters and what works. Since 2001, Agility Consulting has developed a portfolio of assessments that allow leaders to understand their agile capabilities, along with the capabilities of their teams and the organization overall. Such measurement provides leaders with the opportunity to make course corrections on an ongoing basis. But all of that measurement truly comes from one foundation based on The Agile Model®.

THE AGILE MODEL

Focused, Fast & Flexible™

VUCA

I first discovered the value of Leadership Agility Fitness in a VUCA (Volatile, Uncertain, Complex and Ambiguous) environment during my 23 years as a Special Operations Naval Officer responsible for Diving and Explosive Ordnance Disposal teams. These were highly trained, physically and mentally prepared men and women who faced rapidly unfolding and changing circumstances. Now, as an Organizational Psychologist, I have discovered that the key ingredient separating good leaders from best leaders (VUCA Masters) is Leadership Agility Fitness. Current and future trends indicate that organizations are operating in environments characterized by the same or similar VUCA that I experienced in the Navy. Now, as an organizational psychologist and business owner, my earlier observations about the value of leadership agility fitness has been reinforced by not only our work at Agility Consulting but also reinforced by others such as, McKinsey, Deloitte, Harvard Business School, MIT, INSEAD, and London Business School.

Since departing from the Center for Creative Leadership in 2001 and founding Agility Consulting, I focused on researching the topic of AGILITY in organizations and shared the research results through presentations, articles, books, products and services.

I have been singularly focused on studying leadership, team and organizational agility over the past 20 years. This book reflects the integration of leadership agility research, agility consulting client experience and observations, interviews with leaders representing large and small organizations, from a broad distribution of industry sectors reflected in the following organizational clusters (e.g., for profit, not-for-profit, athletics, military, etc.). These data elements are inclusive of my organizational, consulting and military experience of over 40 years to present a framework of leadership agility fitness. When effectively integrated into daily leadership behavior, this plan for leadership agility fitness provides the most effective strategy for leaders to survive and thrive in a very turbulent world today and into the future.

There are significant human and investor costs when an organization is unable to sustain a high level of leadership agility fitness. Not only are investors hurt as more firms face bankruptcy, employees are threatened by their loss of jobs and critical healthcare and retirement benefits. CEOs are confronting more and more challenges as their ability to change their organizations is testing their capability to build a fabric of leadership agility fitness that has sustainability.

Current and future trends indicate that organizations are currently operating in environments characterized by VUCA similar to what I experienced in the Navy. Our most recent example is what the world has experienced with the COVID-19 Global Pandemic in 2020. However, the future will bring additional disruptions for organizations and their leaders. How can leaders build their leadership agility fitness to adapt and thrive in this new world of work characterized by the intensity and frequency of VUCA recently experienced by the COVID-19 Pandemic? Leadership Agility Fitness can best be developed with the creation of a roadmap created as a result of an assessment of a leader's Leadership Agility Fitness strenghs and development needs combined with an individualized development plan.

The actions needed to become a VUCA Master are relevant for both profit and non-profit organization leaders (e.g., C-Suite Executives, Business Unit Executives, Department Head, Project Manager, Agile Coach, etc.).

Tracy Edwards -- VUCA Master

Tracy Edwards represents one of VUCA Masters stories illustrated in this book. Each story is intended to help illustrate how all leaders can effectively demonstrate leadership agility fitness regardless of the disruptive VUCA they face. Edwards demonstrated her ability to master the VUCA (volatility, uncertainty, complexity, and ambiguity) experienced during a global yachting competition.

In 1989, Edwards and her crew faced many challenges that represent the context for organizational leadership today -- relentless changes in the business environments in which they operate. The diversity, intensity, and rapidity of VUCA can challenge leaders on ways to lead effectively during a turbulent environment. Edwards set her sights on a yachting competition, the Whitbread Round the World Race (now known as the Ocean Race), which takes place over nine months and more than 30,000 miles. In addition to the challenges of round-the-world ocean racing, it is very expensive with yachts easily costing more than $1 million. Prior to Edwards and her team, the race was populated by men. The 26-year-old yacht captain, Tracy Edwards, was able to recruit a dozen capable women to join her, along with King Hussein of Jordan to sponsor her team.

The Maiden video documentary combines archival footage from the race and one-on-one interviews with crew members describing their experiences surviving enormous waves in the Southern Ocean, competing against mostly all-male crews and the daily challenges of sharing such tight quarters.

(The VUCA Masters™ Series -- The Tracy Edwards Story | LinkedIn / You can view the brief trailer video for the Maiden documentary produced by Alex Holmes.)

VUCA Masters:
Developing Leadership Agility Fitness for the New World of Work

VUCA Master Capabilities -- Read the brief information in this article and watch the Trailer to the "Maiden" Documentary which will encourage you to watch the entire "Maiden" Documentary. Consider how Edwards demonstrated Leadership Agility (as defined by the following Leadership Agility behaviors):

    1. Anticipate Change -- Identifies future patterns and trends that would impact goal achievement.

    2. Generate Confidence -- Creates an environment of engagement and collaboration of all stakeholders involved in executing the plan.

    3. Initiated Action -- Demonstrated preemptive behavior in all situations.

    4. Liberates Thinking -- Creates an environment where innovation was welcomed.

    5. Evaluate Results -- Assesses the impact of actions on goals and identifies any corrective action needed.

    VUCA Master Webinar or Team Meeting -- Schedule a webinar or team meeting with your team to view the Tracy Edwards brief Maiden video and discuss how Tracy demonstrated Leadership Agility Fitness using the Agility Snapshot provided below. So let's begin by taking a quick snapshot of Tracy Edwards' Leadership Agility Fitness compared to the VUCA she and her team experienced. Very low scores from the Leadership Agility Snapshot can be the result of a low assessment of leadership agility relative to a high level of VUCA. Very high scores on the Leadership Agility Snapshot can be the result of a high assessment of leadership agility relative to a low level of VUCA. Use the Tracy Edwards case to begin your journey of developing your Leadership Agility Fitness and the Leadership Agility Fitness of others.

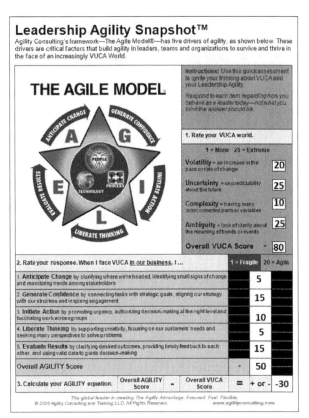

Leadership Agility Snapshot™

Agility Consulting's framework—The Agile Model®—has five drivers of agility, as shown below. These drivers are critical factors that build agility in leaders, teams and organizations to survive and thrive in the face of an increasingly VUCA World.

THE AGILE MODEL

Instructions: Use this quick assessment to ignite your thinking about VUCA and your Leadership Agility.

Respond to each item regarding how you behave as a leader today—not what you think the answer should be.

1. Rate your VUCA world.

1 = None   25 = Extreme

Volatility = an increase in the pace or rate of change	20
Uncertainty = unpredictability about the future	25
Complexity = having many interconnected parts or variables	10
Ambiguity = lack of clarity about the meaning of trends or events	25
Overall VUCA Score =	**80**

2. Rate your response. When I face VUCA in our business, I ...	1 = Fragile 20 = Agile
1. **Anticipate Change** by clarifying where we're headed, identifying small signs of change and monitoring trends among stakeholders	5
2. **Generate Confidence** by connecting tasks with strategic goals, aligning our strategy with our structure and inspiring engagement	15
3. **Initiate Action** by promoting urgency, authorizing decision-making at the right level and facilitating work across groups	10
4. **Liberate Thinking** by supporting creativity, focusing on our customers' needs and seeking many perspectives to solve problems	5
5. **Evaluate Results** by clarifying desired outcomes, providing timely feedback to each other, and using valid data to guide decision-making	15
Overall AGILITY Score =	**50**

3. Calculate your AGILITY equation.	Overall AGILITY Score	-	Overall VUCA Score	= + or -	-30

The global leader in creating The Agility Advantage. Focused. Fast. Flexible.
© 2020 Agility Consulting and Training LLC. All Rights Reserved.   www.agilityconsulting.com

Illustration of using the Leadership Agility Snapshot.

The Illustration provided here (not based on the Tracy Edwards case) reflects an overall VUCA score of 80 out of a possible 100. A Leadership Agility overall score of 50 out of a possible 100 is also reflected here. The overall result is a (-30) score which reflects a significant gap in the leader's agility fitness to address the VUCA disruption. The weaker scores of Anticipate Change and Liberate Thinking could serve as the key areas to focus on for this person's leadership agility development plan. The Practitioner's Guide provides a template for your leadership agility development plan along with developmental recommendations.

Begin Your VUCA Master Journey

Take the time now to complete the Leadership Agility Snapshot on yourself which will serve as the "pre-workout physical" for your Leadership Agility Fitness Plan. A more in-depth Leadership Agility Fitness assessment is available online at *http://agilityconsulting.com/* .

You will find a Leadership Agility Snapshot form on the following page to do a quick assessment of your leadership agility. Consider your experience as a leader during the Covid-19 Pandemic. What VUCA Master strengths did you demonstrate and what capabilities could use further development? In the chapters to follow, you will find additional resources to help guide your planning. In addition, the practitioner guide is intended as a detailed resource guide for you to create your Leadership Agility Fitness development plan.

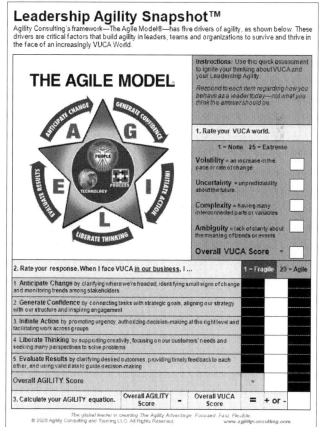

Leadership Agility Snapshot™

Agility Consulting's framework—The Agile Model®—has five drivers of agility, as shown below. These drivers are critical factors that build agility in leaders, teams and organizations to survive and thrive in the face of an increasingly VUCA World.

THE AGILE MODEL

Instructions: Use this quick assessment to ignite your thinking about VUCA and your Leadership Agility

Respond to each item regarding how you behave as a leader today—not what you think the answer should be.

1. Rate your VUCA world.

1 = None 25 = Extreme

Volatility = an increase in the pace or rate of change

Uncertainty = unpredictability about the future

Complexity = having many interconnected parts or variables

Ambiguity = lack of clarity about the meaning of trends or events

Overall VUCA Score =

2. Rate your response. When I face VUCA in our business, I ...	1 – Fragile	20 – Agile
1. Anticipate Change by clarifying where we're headed, identifying small signs of change and monitoring trends among stakeholders		
2. Generate Confidence by connecting tasks with strategic goals, aligning our strategy with our structure and inspiring engagement		
3. Initiate Action by promoting urgency, authorizing decision-making at the right level and facilitating work across groups		
4. Liberate Thinking by supporting creativity, focusing on our customers' needs and seeking many perspectives to solve problems		
5. Evaluate Results by clarifying desired outcomes, providing timely feedback to each other, and using valid data to guide decision-making		
Overall AGILITY Score		=

3. Calculate your AGILITY equation.	Overall AGILITY Score	–	Overall VUCA Score	=	+ or -

The global leader in creating The Agility Advantage: Focused. Fast. Flexible.
© 2020 Agility Consulting and Training LLC. All Rights Reserved.   www.agilityconsulting.com

Nicholas F. Horney, Ph.D.   **29**

VUCA
and the
New World of
Work

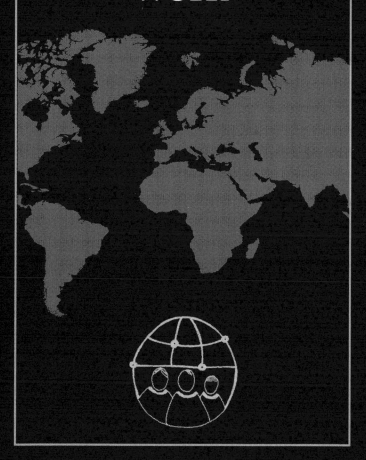

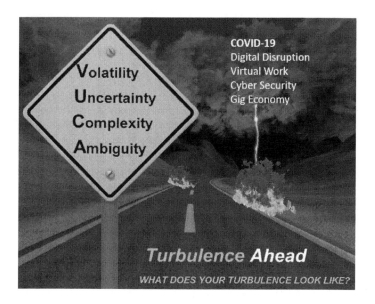

COVID-19
Digital Disruption
Virtual Work
Cyber Security
Gig Economy

Volatility
Uncertainty
Complexity
Ambiguity

Turbulence Ahead

WHAT DOES YOUR TURBULENCE LOOK LIKE?

What is VUCA?

The dynamic and fast-changing nature of our world today is best described by VUCA, a term coined by the US Army War College. VUCA stands for Volatility, Uncertainty, Complexity and Ambiguity. We live now in a VUCA world surrounded by black swans. This is the New Normal. But even within this unpredictably changing world, there are a few important underlying megatrends that will shape our future.

Today, there are almost as many mobile phones in the world as there are people. Digitization is now advancing even more rapidly and fundamentally changing the way business and society work. It presents both opportunities and challenges and the leaders that adapt to this reality will succeed in the future.

Winning in a VUCA world requires the ability to simultaneously manage both leadership short-term and the long-term goals. In turbulent and fast-changing times,

Nicholas F. Horney, Ph.D.   33

leaders need to be anchored in a long-term destination while also dynamically managing the short-term. A leader demonstrating agility must have a clear point of view about the future and build an organization that can navigate towards that destination through good times, and importantly, also in bad times.

Demonstrating leadership agility fitness means having a new kind of leadership mindset and behavior that is values-led and purpose-driven. It means living and breathing those values every day.

Companies that were synonymous with their product categories just a few years ago are now no longer in existence. Kodak, the inventor of the digital camera had to wind up its operations. HMV, the British entertainment retailing company and Borders, once the second largest US bookstore, have shut down due to their inability to evolve their business models with the changing times.

The dynamic and fast-changing nature of our world today is best described by VUCA, a term coined by the US Army War College. VUCA stands for Volatility, Uncertainty, Complexity and Ambiguity.

A Typical VUCA Day for a Global CLO

Let's take a quick look at a typical "VUCA day" in the life of Sam, a Chief Learning Officer for a global consumer products company. Sam's day starts at 4-4:30 AM conducting a conference call from home with a global team from Europe, Asia, India, Mexico, Canada, and US. From 4:30-5:30 AM, Sam reads and responds to the 200 emails she has accumulated over night. After a quick breakfast with her family, she departs for work at 7 AM and makes 3 calls to key managers for updates for the upcoming staff meeting. At 9 AM Sam joins her peers for a staff meeting with her boss, the SVP, Human Resources. At 10 AM, she is interviewed by an executive coach about one of the company's high potential leaders based in Asia but is interrupted by a call from the president of the company's European business unit with a critical talent-related issue. She reschedules the meeting with the executive coach to discuss the HIPO. At 11 AM Sam is involved in a problem-solving meeting with members of her team about the slow progress on a new Learning Management System which is already 3 months behind its scheduled implementation date.

At noon, she has a private lunch with the Chief Operating Officer to discuss the potential impact of the corporate restructuring plan on available global talent and how her learning organization can support the restructuring. Included in their discussion is the learning and experience the company has had complementing full-time employees with part-timers, consultants, suppliers and even customers as part of the broader definition of the company's workforce. The COO also surprises her with a discussion about the talent implications of a potential acquisition in Australia. At 1 PM, she participates in a conference call with professional association colleagues about a national conference presentation that she has been asked to deliver on her company's use of key agility indicators and other metrics to help manage in a very turbulent and uncertain business environment. At 2 PM, Sam meets with a project team of HIPO leaders participating in one of their company's Strategic Leadership Forums to discuss the team's presentation and recommendations for the senior leadership team.

She has to leave the corporate office to attend a 3 PM meeting with the counselor at her daughter's high school. Sam rushes back for a 4:30 PM meeting with the CIO on the leadership development implications of a new leadership dashboard that is being introduced in six months across company. At 6 PM, she has a conference call with GMs across globe introducing the new concept of leaders developing leaders and the role each one will play in its implementation. During her drive home at 8 PM, she makes several calls in her car to follow up on project-related work. After dinner and a glass of wine, Sam settles in for an 11 PM conference call with a pilot project team in Singapore.

During 2019 into early 2020, I worked with a team led by Dr. George Hallenbeck at the Center for Creative Leadership to produce a number of industry sector reports describing the VUCA experienced in each and introduce a new and innovative approach to talent management referred to as Talent Portfolio Agility™. The purpose was to prepare talent solutions for industry sector clients that were focused on the key industry-sector disruptions. We chose the term RUPT (Rapid, Unpredictable, Paradoxical and Tangled) to establish a unique brand which reflected the disruptions impacting the industry. I have provided a brief summary of what was discovered in each of these reports.

VUCA in the Healthcare Industry

With the healthcare marketplace transforming to a value-based reimbursement model, healthcare organizations are aiming for efficiency, cost control and sustainability by rethinking their strategy and reallocating capital and resources toward future business models, either through investments in technology or different care delivery models. Turbulent disruptions are occurring, not only in regulations but also in four other significant areas: technology (artificial intelligence, machine learning and cybersecurity), consumer-related (rapidly rising consumer expectations and the digital consumer), society-related (society is grappling with an opioid crisis) and industry-related changes (value-based pricing, mergers and acquisitions (M&As), and specialty drug pricing and supply chain disruption). These disruptions are breaking existing silos and redefining the basis of competition. In an industry rife with continued disruption, companies will need to become more agile in order to take advantage of critical growth opportunities or risk falling behind as competitors bolster their positions and reshape the healthcare value chain. The agility of your talent portfolio and hence ability to adapt and thrive in the face of continuous disruptions in the business environment is dependent on your organization's talent portfolio agility mindset, process and people.

Talent Portfolio Agility™
RUPT™ Report for Healthcare

Disruptive Trends Impacting the Healthcare Industry
and Their Implications for Talent
February, 2019
Dr. Nick Horney & Dr. George Hallenbeck

VUCA in the Financial Services Industry

The Financial Services Industry is going through a massive transformation, challenging the way Financial Services Institutions operate, lead and compete on multiple fronts. As a result, Financial Services Firms are rethinking their strategy and exploring new business models, either through investments in technology or partnering with FinTech firms to create new ecosystems to meet changing client requirements. Turbulent disruptions are occurring in four significant areas: client-related (due to changing client expectations); technology (new FinTech market players, new technologies and cybersecurity); industry-related [consolidation through mergers and acquisitions (M&As), new organization structures and the war for talent] and societal (enhanced regulations, reporting requirements and responsible corporate citizenship). These disruptions are breaking existing silos and redefining the basis of competition. In order to stay competitive, Financial Services Organizations need to be more agile if they are going to survive in this rapidly changing, technology-driven marketplace. The last several years have shown that Financial Services Organizations need to be ready for anything. To be competitive they will need to provide client-centric products and services, leverage and excel in new technologies, build and sustain ecosystems, be active in their communities, keep ahead of changing regulations, and balance the need to be more transparent and secure at the same time. Your ability to transform into a modern, digital Financial Service Organization is dependent on your organization's talent portfolio agility mindset, process and skills.

Talent Portfolio Agility™
RUPT™ Report for Financial Services

March, 2019
Dr. Nick Horney, Diane Reinhold, MBA & Dr. George Hallenbeck

VUCA in the Talent Management Services Industry

The Talent Management Services (TMS) industry is going through a massive transformation, challenging the way TMS firms operate and dramatically changing their products and services. The TMS industry has always been responsible for acquiring and retaining talent, onboarding new hires and performance management. Today, however, TMS firms' portfolios need to include talent strategies that drive business strategies, workforce planning, leadership development and succession, talent analytics, and diversity and inclusion. Many large consulting firms are joining the already crowded space of small consulting firms, training providers and universities. As a result, TMS firms are rethinking their strategies and exploring new business models, either through investments in technology or partnering with other providers to create a more comprehensive portfolio to meet changing client requirements. Turbulent disruptions are occurring in four significant areas: client-related (new world of work, organizational culture); technology (big data and people analytics, automation anxiety and new talent platforms); industry-related [reinvention of talent processes, new and larger competitors and emphasis on return on investment (ROI)]; and societal (worker's market, diversity and inclusion, and responsible corporate citizenship). These disruptions are breaking existing silos and redefining the basis of competition. In order to stay competitive, TMS firms need to be more agile if they are going to survive in this rapidly changing, technology-driven marketplace. The last several years have shown that TMS organizations need to be preemptive and resilient when dealing with continuous change.

To be competitive, TMS firms will need to effectively sense and respond to the disruptive marketplace by:

- providing client-centric products and services;
- leveraging and excelling in new technologies;
- building and sustaining partnership ecosystems to widen their offerings;
- actively influencing and impacting stakeholders; and
- balancing the need to be more fluid while sustaining appropriate structure at the same time. A TMS organization's ability to achieve a competitive advantage in this disruptive business environment is dependent on the organization's talent portfolio agility (TPA) mindset, processes and people.

Talent Portfolio Agility™
RUPT™ Report for
Talent Management Services

Disruptive Trends Impacting Talent Management Services
and Their Implications for Talent
April, 2019
Dr. Nick Horney, Dr. George Hallenbeck & Diane Reinhold, MBA.

New World of Work and Implications for Talent

The World of Work is going through a massive transformation, challenging the way organizations operate and dramatically changing how they manage their talent. Organizations have always needed to acquire and retain talent, onboard new hires and manage their performance. Today, however, organizations need talent strategies that support ever evolving business needs. As technology enables new business models, many organizations are facing new competitors, including one-stop behemoths and small, nimble start-ups – forcing them to respond in new and different ways. As a result, organizations require new types of talent to support these new business models, and must explore new ways to find and engage that talent. This massive transformation of the World of Work is driven by disruptions in four significant areas: Client-related (rise of the digital consumer, demand for one-stop convenience, and demand for more customization); Digital (new technologies, big data & data analytics, and cybersecurity); Industry-related (consolidation, boutiques & start-ups, ecosystems, and war for talent); and Societal / Global (new world of work, regulatory pressure, responsible corporate citizenship, and diversity & inclusion). These disruptions are breaking existing silos and redefining the basis of competition. In order to stay competitive and survive in this rapidly changing marketplace, organizations need to be more agile.

The last several years have shown that organizations need to be preemptive and resilient when dealing with continuous change. To continue to thrive, organizations will need to effectively sense and respond to the disruptive marketplace by:

• Providing client-centric products and services;

• Leveraging and excelling in new technologies;

• Building and sustaining partnership ecosystems to widen their offerings;
• Actively influencing and impacting stakeholders; and
• Balancing the need to be more fluid while sustaining appropriate structure at the same time.

An organization's ability to achieve a sustainable advantage in this disruptive business environment is dependent on the organization's talent portfolio agility (TPA) mindset, processes and people.

Talent Portfolio Agility™
RUPT™ Report

The New World of Work and
Its Implications for Talent

March 2020
Diane Reinhold, MBA, Dr. Nick Horney, & Dr. George Hallenbeck

VUCA Prime

My business partner, Tom O'Shea, shared an overview of Bob Johansen's concept of VUCA Prime in one of Tom's Agility blogs. "A few years ago Bob Johansen, distinguished fellow at the Institute for the Future, developed an effective leadership framework as a "VUCA counterweight" he called VUCA PRIME. Kirk Lawrence, Executive Education Program Director at the UNC-CH Kenan-Flagler School of Business, does a good job of outlining the VUCA/VUCA Prime leadership corollaries in a white paper entitled LEADING IN A VUCA WORLD. Lawrence also extensively references a People & Strategy Journal article that ACT Partner Nick Horney and I wrote with Bill Pasmore, Columbia University Professor and SVP at the Center for Creative Leadership back in 2010 ..."Leadership Agility: A Business Imperative for a VUCA World" that provides additional valuable insights.

Johansen's VUCA PRIME (VP) calls for leaders to focus on building Vision, Understanding, Clarity and Agility as the pathway to coping and overcoming the daunting and somewhat paralyzing impacts of the VUCA WORLD. I would go so far as even suggesting that VP represents the core of a real executive job description and key accountabilities. Johansen says, Volatility can be countered with Vision as leaders provide and reinforce the way forward and navigate the turbulence to achieve success. As any good skipper knows, you always strive to define your point of sail by compass setting or a fixed landmark to help guide helmsmen and crew ... no matter the conditions.

Vision requires explicitness to answer the seminal three questions ... Why are we here? How will we be successful? What are our success measures? From Vision comes the opportunity to transform Uncertainty to Understanding bringing all team members into a shared mindset and understanding of how they can contribute to success along with the key operating principles that will promote active communication and widespread involvement practices. As with any transformation that aims to shape new individual and team behaviors, continual and consistent two-way communication is essential. It's not just talking at folks - it must involve active listening to gain as well as give understanding. Capturing the key elements of Vision to include core values, strategies and success measures into a broadly communicated and engaged Strategy Map that is alive, interactive and dynamic helps fuel continual understanding ... it is not a once and done campaign. It is a living, breathing and intrinsic way of leading and believing.

Complexity can be countered by Clarity that comes from building disciplines around the core basics, constantly reinforcing the real priorities and avoiding the cul-de-sacs of non-value added activities. Dedication to being truly customer-centric and staying connected to giving and receiving internal and external customer feedback can eradicate unnecessary complexity. The VUCA world brings tremendous complexity everyday - so organizations must be mindful of not creating mountains of internal complexity and keep a shared commitment to simplicity. Clarity can come from re-examining and rebooting your meeting regimens and ownership (why does it exist and who responsible for its quality?). A major opportunity area to reduce complexity and increase clarity relates to your internal information and data integrity. How many versions of the "truth" exist within your organization. I have one client that recently concluded they needed to call for "TRUTH SUMMIT" ... a collaborative workday with cross-functional "senators" tasked to define "one version of the truth" so all functions can work off the same set of assumptions. Sure would be useful in Washington these days.

Finally, Ambiguity can be countered with Agility! Changing the metronome of organizational cadence from a slow "schmaltzy" waltz to more of a riverdance-like jig (like at my recent St. Pat's Party) will help invigorate the energy to search and destroy the swamps of ambiguity that we often tolerate by creating a faster iteration cycle to sense and respond throughout the organization.

Here is where THE AGILE MODEL® kicks into bring a real roadmap for building agility. Organizations that systematically examine, measure (e.g. using our AGILITY ANALYTICS) and then strengthen leadership and organizational behaviors using our development guides, coaching and interactive workshops find themselves in a position to make their AGILITY a competitive advantage in this increasing fast-paced VUCA WORLD. Agility with your leaders, teams and business units can be effectively measured and charted using visual heat-maps to clearly highlight and locate your gaps

VUCA Masters:
Developing Leadership Agility Fitness for the New World of Work

Then there was COVID-19 Pandemic in 2020 – 2021 which impacted all countries and created global disruptions appropriately characterized by the term VUCA. COVID-19 rapidly accelerated many of the changes that were already disrupting the business world, e.g., gig economy, digital disruption, etc., which characterized the New World of Work.

New World of Work

The Covid-19 Pandemic accelerated the implementation of many elements of the New World of Work which had been transforming business operations over the past couple of decades. In fact, I collaborated on an article published a decade ago entitled, "Leadership Agility: A Business Imperative for a VUCA World." (Horney, Pasmore and O'Shea, 2010) In today's world, the structure, content, and process of work have changed. Work is now:

- more cognitively complex
- more team-based and collaborative
- more dependent on social skills
- more dependent on technological competence
- more time pressured
- more mobile and less dependent on geography.

In today's world, you are likely working for an organization that is very different due to competitive pressures and technological breakthroughs. Organizations today are:

- leaner and more agile

- more focused on identifying value from the customer perspective

- more tuned to dynamic competitive requirements and strategy

- less hierarchical in structure and decision authority

- less likely to provide lifelong careers and job security

- continually reorganizing to maintain or gain competitive advantage.

Key organizational changes characterizing the New World of Work include:

Nicholas F. Horney, Ph.D.   43

• **Reduced hierarchical structure**—Hierarchies are cumbersome and cannot respond quickly to changing market demands, such as pressures for reduced cycle time and continuous innovation. Hierarchies are being replaced by cross unit organizational groupings with fewer layers and more decentralized decision making.

• **Blurred boundaries**—As organizations become more laterally structured, boundaries begin to breakdown as different parts of the organization need to work more effectively together. Boundaries between departments as well as between job categories (manager, professional, technical) become looser and there is a greater need for task and knowledge sharing.

• **Teams as basic building blocks**—The move toward a team-based organizational structure results from pressures to make rapid decisions, to reduce inefficiencies, and to continually improve work processes.

• **New management perspective**—Workers are no longer managed to comply with rules and orders, but rather to be committed to organizational goals and mission. The blurring of boundaries also affects organizational roles. As employees gain more decision authority and latitude, managers become more social supporters and coaches rather than commanders.

• **Continuous change**—Organizations are expected to continue the cycles of reflection and reorganization. However, changes may be both large and small and are likely to be interspersed with periods of stability.

Over the past two decades, a new pattern of work is emerging as the knowledge economy realizes the full potential of both new technologies and new organizational models. The changes fall into the following domains:

• Cognitive competence

• Social and interactive competence

• The new "psychological contract" between employees and employers

• Changes in process and place

Although these domains are discussed separately, they overlap. We briefly discuss the overlaps, where they exist, and point to the benefits and concerns the new work patterns present for workers and managers.

COGNITIVE COMPETENCE

Cognitive workers are expected to be more functionally and cognitively fluid and able to work across many kinds of tasks and situations. The broader span of work, brought about by changes in organizational structure, also creates new demands, including:

• Increased complexity of work—Workers need to know more, not only to do their jobs and tasks, but also to work effectively with others on teams. Many knowledge-based tasks require sound analytical and judgment skills to carry out work that is more novel, extemporaneous, and context based, with few rules and structured ways of working. Although demand for high cognitive skills are especially prominent in professional, technical, and managerial jobs, even administrative tasks require more independent decision making and operational decision making.

• Continuous competency development—Not only do workers need to keep their technology skills up to date, they need to be continuous learners in their knowledge fields and to also be more conversant with business strategy. Time to read and attend training classes is no longer a perquisite of only a few, it is essential for all workers.

• Different ways of thinking—Rosabeth Kantor argues that cross-functional and cross boundary teams require "kaleidoscope thinking," the ability to see alternative angles and perspectives and to create new patterns of thinking that propel innovation. Workers also need to be able to synthesize disparate ideas in order to make the cognitive leaps that underlie innovation.

COGNITIVE OVERLOAD: THE COST OF COMPLEXITY

Vastly increased access to information has made work both easier and more difficult. The ease comes from ability to rapidly locate and download information from diverse web sites. The difficulty comes with the need to consume and make sense of new information in a timely fashion. Information overload, coupled with time pressures and increased work complexity, lead to what psychologists call "cognitive overload syndrome (COS)." Symptoms of COS include stress, inability to concentrate, multitasking, task switching, and a tendency to focus on what is easy to do quickly rather than what is important.

Nicholas F. Horney, Ph.D.   45

SOCIAL AND INTERACTIVE COMPETENCE

In a 2001 report on the changing nature of work, the National Research Council called attention to the importance of relational and interactive aspects of work. As collaboration and collective activity become more prevalent, workers need well-developed social skills—what the report calls "emotional labor."

Good social skills are necessary for:

• **Team work and collaboration**—Conflict resolution and negotiation skills are essential to collaborative work. Conflicts often occur about group goals, work methods, assignments, workloads, and recognition. Team members with good conflict and negotiation skills are better equipped to deal openly with problems, to listen and understand different perspectives, and to resolve issues in mutually beneficial ways.

• **Relationship development and networking**—Sharing important information, fulfilling promises, willingness to be influenced, and listening are building blocks of reciprocity and the development of trust. When workers trust one another, they are more committed to attaining mutual goals, more likely to help one another through difficulties, and more willing to share and develop new ideas.

• **Learning and growth**—Many organizations strive to be learning centers—to create conditions in which employees learn not only through formal training but through relationships with coworkers. Learning relationships build on joint problem solving, insight sharing, learning from mistakes, and working closely together to aid transmission of tacit knowledge. Learning also develops from mentoring relationships between newcomers and those with experience and organizational know-how.

THE COSTS OF COLLABORATIVE ENVIRONMENTS

In a collaborative work setting, the fate of individuals is inextricably bound to collective success. Dependence on others for one's own success is often uncomfortable. As Susan Mohrman and Susan Cohen write in a chapter from The Changing Nature of Work:

"We have been socialized to value individual responsibility and individual achievement, and feel discomfort with the thought of relying on others."

Comments about the fear of not having individual efforts recognized are common in the literature on team work.

Collaboration and relationship development also take time and effort. Understanding coworkers' perspectives and "thought worlds" requires time spent listening, integrating, and synthesizing. For those workers recognized as both knowledgeable and approachable, the demands of interaction may be especially high.

C. The New Psychological Contract
As work changes, so does the nature of the relationships between employees and employers. In the new work context, the informal, "psychological contract" between workers and employers—what each expects of the other—focuses on competency development, continuous training, and work/life balance. In contrast, the old psychological contract was all about job security and steady advancement within the firm. As already discussed, few workers expect, or desire, lifelong employment in a single firm.

D. The Changing Workplace
The changing workplace is driven by the organizational issues described above and enabled by technologies that support mobility and easy access to information. These pressures and opportunities, however, have not resulted in a specific new workplace model. Many models and ideas exist concurrently, with designs depending upon the organization, its work practices, culture, and customers. The table below key drivers, solutions, and potential issues raised by the solution.

Nicholas F. Horney, Ph.D.   47

Table 1. Drivers, Solutions, and Issues for the Changing Workplace

DRIVERS	WORKPLACE AND TECHNOLOGY SOLUTIONS	ISSUES AND CONCERNS
Increased use of teams and cross unit work; more pressure for communication and information flow	• More meeting space • Greater variety of meeting spaces (open & enclosed, large & small) • Smaller individual workspaces • More open individual workspaces • Unassigned workspaces • Greater interior visibility to support awareness • Mobile supports (phones, laptops, PDAs, wireless) • Personal video, instant messaging, desktop team software • More use of project rooms • Displayed information and work progress • Small rooms for individual focus • Lockers for personal belongings	• Increased noise • Increased distractions and interruptions • Potential for 'over communicating' • Cultural barriers to behavioral change • Individuals working longer hours to compensate for lack of time to do individual tasks • Expectations that workers are always available
Greater use of dispersed work groups—often global	• Increased use of video conferencing, computer-based team tools • More reliance on conference calls • Greater need for mobile technological supports for meeting rooms • Use of facilities beyond normal working hours	• Expansion of the workday to accommodate geographically dispersed team meetings • Loss of opportunity to develop trust through face to face interaction • More difficulty managing and coordinating • Very high dependence on technological reliability
Continual reorganization and restructuring	• Flexible infrastructure to support rapid reconfiguration • Mobile furnishings	• Acoustical problems with loss of good enclosure • Potential for reduced ergonomic effectiveness
Reduced costs/more efficient space use	• Shared or unassigned workspaces • Centralized filing system • Reduced workstation size and increased overall densities • Greater overall spatial variety to enable different kinds of work to be accommodated at same time	• Increased distractions and interruptions • Increased noise • May meet with employee resistance • More difficult for paper intensive work
Improved quality of work life and attraction of new workers	• More equitable access to daylight, views, and other amenities • More equitable spatial allocation and workspace features • Amenities for stress reduction and quiet relaxation	• Resistance from those who support hierarchical space allocation

VUCA Masters:
Developing Leadership Agility Fitness for the New World of Work

During the COVID-19 Pandemic, many organizations redefined how work would be done (illustrations from a recent leadership agility webinar):

- Virtual work
- Use of Microsoft Teams or Zoom for meetings
- Contract signatures
- Contactless payments
- New safety measures
- Performance reviews
- Leadership of virtual teams
- Greater cybersecurity challenges
- Teams composed of full-time, part-time, gig workers, etc.

Impact of COVID-19 on people's livelihoods, their health and our food systems

Joint statement by ILO, FAO, IFAD and WHO (October 13, 2020)

The COVID-19 pandemic has led to a dramatic loss of human life worldwide and presents an unprecedented challenge to public health, food systems and the world of work. The economic and social disruption caused by the pandemic is devastating: tens of millions of people are at risk of falling into extreme poverty, while the number of undernourished people, currently estimated at nearly 690 million, could increase by up to 132 million by the end of the year.

Millions of enterprises face an existential threat. Nearly half of the world's 3.3 billion global workforce are at risk of losing their livelihoods. Informal economy workers are particularly vulnerable because the majority lack social protection and access to quality health care and have lost access to productive assets. Without the means to earn an income during lockdowns, many are unable to feed themselves and their families. For most, no income means no food, or, at best, less food and less nutritious food.

The pandemic has been affecting the entire food system and has laid bare its fragility. Border closures, trade restrictions and confinement measures have been preventing farmers from accessing markets, including for buying inputs and selling their produce, and agricultural workers from harvesting crops, thus disrupting domestic and international food supply chains and reducing access to healthy, safe and diverse diets. The pandemic has decimated jobs and placed millions of livelihoods at risk. As breadwinners lose jobs, fall ill and die, the food security and nutrition of millions of women and men are under threat, with those in low-income countries, particularly the most marginalized populations, which include small-scale farmers and indigenous peoples, being hardest hit.

Millions of agricultural workers – waged and self-employed – while feeding the world, regularly face high levels of working poverty, malnutrition and poor health, and suffer from a lack of safety and labour protection as well as other types of abuse. With low and irregular incomes and a lack of social support, many of them are spurred to continue working, often in unsafe conditions, thus exposing themselves and their families to additional risks. Further, when experiencing income losses, they may resort to negative coping strategies, such as distress sale of assets, predatory loans or child labour. Migrant agricultural workers are particularly vulnerable, because they face risks in their transport, working and living conditions and struggle to access support measures put in place by governments. Guaranteeing the safety and health of all agri-food workers – from primary producers to those involved in food processing, transport and retail, including street food vendors – as well as better incomes and protection, will be critical to saving lives and protecting public health, people's livelihoods and food security.

In the COVID-19 crisis food security, public health, and employment and labour issues, in particular workers' health and safety, converge. Adhering to workplace safety and health practices and ensuring access to decent work and the protection of labour rights in all industries will be crucial in addressing the human dimension of the crisis. Immediate and purposeful action to save lives and livelihoods should include extending social protection towards universal health coverage and income support for those most affected. These include workers in the informal economy and in poorly protected and low-paid jobs, including youth, older workers, and migrants. Particular attention must be paid to the situation of women, who are over-represented in low-paid jobs and care roles. Different forms of support are key, including cash transfers, child allowances and healthy school meals, shelter and food relief initiatives, support for employment retention and recovery, and financial relief for businesses, including micro, small and medium-sized enterprises. In designing and implementing such measures it is essential that governments work closely with employers and workers.

Countries dealing with existing humanitarian crises or emergencies are particularly exposed to the effects of COVID-19. Responding swiftly to the pandemic, while ensuring that humanitarian and recovery assistance reaches those most in need, is critical..

By applying a tool, Imagility(TM), which can be found at *AgilityConsulting.com*, you can rapidly work with your team to identify its turbulence.

What Does Your Turbulence Look Like?

1. *Select 2-3 Images that best describe the turbulence (changes) that your organization is currently facing or will face in the future.*
2. *Post-it Notes – Write a phrase describing this turbulence on a post-it and attach it adjacent to the image selected.*
3. *Group Debrief – Share your turbulence images and what they represent, your name, organization and role in your organization.*

Interactive Exercise to Identify VUCA

Matt Stevens – VUCA Master

Matt Stevens transitioned from the U.S. Navy in July 2017 after serving for 26 years as a SEAL. He attended The Honor Foundation's (THF) inaugural East Coast class in the Spring of 2016, joined the THF SOF Advisory Board in the Spring of 2017, and then joined THF's Board of Directors in February 2018. Throughout his career, Matt served as a Special Operations Executive leading high-performing teams conducting our nation's most sensitive operations, cultivating interagency relationships and executing plans in dynamic environments. A native of Charlotte, NC, Matt graduated from U.S. Naval Academy in 1991 with a B.S. in Ocean Engineering. He graduated Basic Underwater Demolition/SEAL (BUD/S) training in 1992 with class 179 and was subsequently assigned to the East Coast where he served in various SEAL Teams, SEAL Delivery Vehicle Teams and Naval Special Warfare Development Group (NSWDG) Matt commanded at every level in the Naval Special Warfare Community to include a Squadron at NSWDG, SEAL Team TWO, Naval Special Warfare Unit THREE, and Naval Special Warfare Group FOUR. He served staff tours at the Joint Special Operations Command in Fort Bragg, NC; as the Operations Officer at Naval Special Warfare Group TWO in Virginia Beach, VA; and in the Office of the Assistant Secretary of Defense for Special Operations and Low-Intensity Conflict (ASD SO/LIC) in the Pentagon. Matt served on the leadership team of an emerging technology company from 2017-2019 before assuming the role of Chief Executive Officer of THF

Agility
and
The Agile Model

Leadership Agility serves as one of the foundational elements of the Domains of Business Agility represented by the Business Agility Institute. "The three domains under the Leadership Dimension which govern how to shape an agile organization. People Management defines the role of managers as leaders who, among many other things, engage, empower, delegate, coach, and inspire. One Team defines a culture of collaboration underpinned by communication and transparency across individuals, teams, and divisions. And Strategic Agility shapes how an agile organization sets, communicates and operationalizes an adaptive market vision." (Domains of Business Agility) These domains align very well with the Drivers represented in The AGILE Model®. (The Agile Model® | Agility Consulting)

Each Leadership Agility Fitness Driver, as defined by The AGILE Model®, is a vital force, yet each one alone can't elevate a leader to maximizing his/her potential to be a VUCA Master. For example, having a focused effort on Anticipating Change does little to demonstrate VUCA Mastery if there is not a sense of urgency to Initiate Action based on the trends and patterns of changes anticipated through the deliberate enhancement of marketplace monitoring tools. Nor can a leadership initiative to Generate Confidence in all employees through an employee engagement survey achieve VUCA Mastery without providing employees with a line-of-sight understanding of the business strategy and a culture supportive of Liberated Thinking. VUCA Mastery relies on the mutual reinforcement and alignment of all five Drivers. If there are major inconsistencies, the leader may only achieve limited success. On the other hand, if the five Drivers work together, the leader would be able to continuously learn and create value, regardless of changes in the marketplace.

Nicholas F. Horney, Ph.D. 57

The Agile Model® was derived from multidisciplinary research from the public and private sectors in the areas of Total Quality Management (e.g., Malcolm Baldrige National Quality Award), Manufacturing Agility (e.g., Agility Forum), Confidence (e.g., Rosebeth Moss Kanter), Employee Engagement (e.g., The Gallup Organization, Kennexa, etc.), Innovation (e.g., Center for Creative Leadership), and Predictive Analytics (e.g., Thomas Davenport). Academic research from Dr. Lee Dyer (Cornell), Dr. Don Sull (London Business School), Dr. Ed Lawler (USC) and Dr. Yves Doz (INSEAD) provided many of the theoretical underpinnings for the LAP.

THE AGILE MODEL®   DomAins of Business Agility

Independent research by organizational psychologists at an organizational research firm was conducted on the Agile Model's psychometric properties and provided evidence of the reliability and validity of the Leadership Agility Profile™ (LAP) assessment. When factor analyzed, the five drivers of the LAP (Anticipate Change, Generate Confidence, Initiate Action, Liberate Thinking and Evaluate Results) are distinct factors and highly reliable. Also, when regressing the outcome-related items on A-G-I-L-E factors, the factors account for 60% of the variance. The LAP has a reliable scale of five distinct factors (each with a Coefficient Alpha above .90 where .75 is the minimum required to demonstrate reliability). The research also indicated that the outcome related items had a Coefficient Alpha of .819.

The following is an overview of the five Drivers of The Agile Model®.

Anticipate Change

Change is the new normal operating context that is synchronous and disruptive with all of the VUCA factors percolating a challenging new brew every day. Unexpected events occur, expected ones don't, and conditions vary significantly. Change is something that no one, and no organization, can ignore. If all is going well, people fear change. If things are not going well, people hope for change. Either way, in your role as a leader, you need to deal with it.

The best way to deal with change is through clear-eyed anticipation. Anticipating change has become a rigorous endeavor for those serious about staying competitive in a rapidly changing global environment. Professor Don Sull from the MIT Sloan School of Management describes the current corporate visibility or capability to see into the future in his book, The Upside of Turbulence as the fog of the future where all knowledge is provisional. What he means is the world has become sufficiently volatile and uncertain and the past paradigms used to guide our actions are only provisionally valid to help navigate in today's increasingly foggy future. Sull is very clear in saying, "Not only do we not know what the future holds, . . . we can't know what the future holds," and trying to predict too far out can cause some seriously bad decisions. The key to driving consistently reliable execution is to create a shared belief system or culture within your organization that excels in sensing and responding better and faster to the rapidly changing conditions.

Technology, globalization, demographics, security, and consumer demand for choices all contribute to making today's society one of accelerating change. More recently, the Covid-19 Pandemic demonstrated how well we were prepared, or ill-prepared, for such a comprehensive change. The drivers of change are numerous and complex, and their impact varies from one business sector to another. As a leader, adapting too late or too little can result in radical measures such as large-scale downsizing, hostile take-overs, rushed mergers can result in consequences such as accelerated obsolescence. In today's unstable economic climate resulting from Covid-19, leaders that succeed in integrating agility into their business strategy in an informed way will have a competitive advantage. Anticipating change is not just building foresight and anticipation to identify possible future scenarios as a first step in preparing for change and managing it successfully. These steps are important, but agility is much more fluid and dynamic in striving to create your team's capabilities to sense and respond better and faster.

The fluidity in your capability to anticipate change will contribute greatly to your success at minimizing obstacles and resistance in your team's mindset that could limit the agility of your team.

Anticipating change isn't predicting the future or predicting the unpredictable. In fact, it derives from the ability to project what is expected and to thereby see the forces of change and how those forces might play out. Anticipating change depends on having a clear understanding of your team, and then identifying the conditions and forces that affect it, projecting how these will interact in dynamic ways, and envisioning various outcomes. As forces and conditions change, so will outcomes. The paradigm shift for leaders is the realization that they cannot predict a singular, specific view of the future. The real point of competitive differentiation comes to those leaders who can engage their teams in a dynamic, super-sensory body by building widespread capability for understanding forces of change at all levels—in both personal and corporate ways.

Generate Confidence

Confidence is something that seems to be in short supply these days, across our country and the rest of the world. Remember when elected leaders and major financial institutions actually engendered high trust and confidence? We now live in an era where our confidence and trust in elected leaders and major institutions are at an all-time low. The volatility and uncertainty we face each day erodes our sense of confidence. Research clearly shows that confidence is strongly linked to individual, team, organizational, and even national productivity and sense of well-being. In our hyper-turbulent world, it is amazing how fast confidence can crash but also, with the power of social networking, how fast it can grow. Increasing confidence is a significant goal of many leadership efforts to improve team climate and culture. Generating confidence with all team members is a direct and comprehensible goal worthy of systematic effort of action and measurement. A VUCA Master will have a total stakeholder orientation that includes customers, suppliers, consumers, communities, and owners too.

Confidence is one of those hard-to-measure, yet extraordinarily important, dynamics. Just rewind your memory over the past few years to find a world full of examples of lost confidence—consumer confidence, corporate uncertainties, geopolitical and societal disillusionment. From these examples and more, you can see the impact that lost confidence has on the economic well-being and attitudes of whole countries, corporations, regions, and individuals.

Initiate Action

The growing pace and complexity of the business environment will continue to bring extraordinary stress and pressure on leadership for most organizations and will be increasingly destructive for those leaders that continue to try and use hierarchical, command-and-control decision-making and management practices. Although this growing complexity and pace creates challenges for all leaders, it also creates a great opportunity for differentiation and competitive advantage. Leaders who are able to build superior skill in sensing and responding better and faster, especially in developing high-performance collaborative teams talented in those skills, will be creating real, sustainable advantages for success and personal growth.

Liberate Thinking

Any leader responsible for running a business supplying consumer products to retailers will tell you that you had better be inventing your next innovation even before you've launched your latest innovation on the retail floor. Retailers and consumers have an insatiable appetite for newer, better products, generally at lower prices, with a better carbon footprint and more features than before. How can leaders survive with this aggressive expectation for continuous change and reinvention? Perhaps the more important question is how you'll survive if you don't create the culture and expectation in your team for this kind of fresh, innovative thinking. The key for leaders is to create a team environment for innovation and fresh thinking. The world has indeed become flat with new ideas and better products coming from all corners of the world faster than ever. It is a matter of fitness, and just as in the Olympics, those with the greatest skills related to the critical events will emerge as the world champions.

Evaluate Results

There is truth in the old business proverb that what gets measured gets done. Yet one of the many challenges business leaders face in today's fast-paced, change-driven world is determining the "what and how" of measuring relevant organizational performance. Traditional outcome metrics—sales, profits, costs, employee retention, and even customer satisfaction—are important, if not essential. But if they are the only performance measures in your scorecard, you may be navigating your team by looking out the rear window instead of looking forward.

The pace of change, rampant innovation, and rising customer expectation at all levels demand a different and more fluid approach to performance measurement. Getting desired results is the goal of all high performing teams, and the classic way of determining if results are achieved is evaluation. Many think of evaluation primarily in terms of measurement. It is also a way of determining what was done wrong, if results aren't achieved, and what could have been done differently. Technology has enabled more dynamic, interactive, and real-time capabilities that support nimble and adaptive organizations.

Illustration of how a Fortune 50 company focuses on Strategic Agility as part of its performance management process.

> **Strategic Agility** is the ability to learn quickly and leverage a flexible mindset in response to shifting dynamics, adversity, and/or change. Outstanding leaders are frustrated by an acceptance of the status quo and instead continually push themselves, their teams, and their businesses to learn, to generate new ideas, and (at times) to take needed risks to position ABC Co. favorably in the marketplace.

*   Does this individual respond to the pressure of constant change by eagerly re-examining how they, their team, and the business may need to adapt and best respond to opportunities or challenges ?

LEVELS	BEHAVIORAL DESCRIPTORS
1. Shifts own approach and perspective	Continually examines own behaviors and perspectives in light of dynamic landscape
	Embraces complex or first time problems as opportunities to learn and incorporate new skills into repertoire
	Learns from experience and flexes styles based on immediate needs
2. Assists others in adapting to change	Helps others understand the rationale and positive impact of change by clarifying context or reasons
	Partners with others (e.g., peers, teams, customers/clients, etc.) to explore implications of shifting dynamics and determination of ABC Co.'ss best response
3. Challenges the status quo	Publicly questions "business as usual" approaches by comparing current practices against ABC Co.'s strategic intent and external best practices
	Constructively challenges organizational paradigms, norms, and team members (peers and/or those at higher levels) to consider changes that will foster long-term, sustainable growth and competitiveness
	Encourages others to challenge the status quo
4. Creates and promotes breakthrough insights	Develops "outside the box" concepts that are not obvious to others and are not learned from previous experience
	Re-conceptualizes issues to create innovative ideas that have not been thought of before
	Suggests creative solutions to problems that may involve a tolerance for short-term calculated risk in order to achieve a longer-term payoff or organization-wide (i.e., cross-LOB or cross-geography) achievement and accomplishment

Target Level

Leadership Agility Research

Imagine taking Clausewitz's quote above and replacing the word "war" with the name of your organization. Then replace "a general in time of war is" with "we are."

With a little thought, this quote from about 200 years ago likely sounds something like your day at work. Our research and experience working with executives suggests that it probably does. Competing initiatives, murky strategic priorities, shifting customer preferences, technological advances and managing the unexpected have become normal for today's leaders. And apparently agility—which is really what Clausewitz was talking about when he described the need for a form of flexibility that's disciplined by focus and speed—mattered to military commanders centuries ago.

So if you're wondering if agility will remain relevant and have staying power, we have an answer. That's easy. Agility will remain important for about the next 5 billion years, when our sun will expand and envelop earth's orbit.

The truth, of course, is that thriving as a leader and as an organization depends on the ability to sense and respond to the external environment—an environment fraught with shifting realities and ambiguity. We're finding that the question of "why agility matters" isn't that difficult to answer. In fact, we're finding it increasingly the case that top leaders come to us knowing that agility matters. That's a given. Instead, they come to us for specific guidance regarding how to transform themselves, those around them and their entire organizations into agile entities.

A valuable question to ask, then, is "how" agility matters. Knowing that provides critical insights into the ways in which we assess and develop agility in ourselves and our organizations. And in the sections that follow, you'll find an overview of agility and its supporting processes. That section provides the context for understanding both how we conceptualize agility and how we measure it. Next, we'll focus on what we found when we analyzed data gathered from 1,078 leaders using one of our assessments. The final section deals with distilling those findings into specific lessons learned and action steps to consider.

Nicholas F. Horney, Ph.D.   63

The Specific Nature of Agility

In our experience, agility demands competence in a number of specific capabilities as outlined in The Agile Model®. Those specific capabilities stem from multiple disciplines of academic research, best practices from numerous organizations and industries, and our practical experience in determining what matters and what works. And over the years we've developed a portfolio of assessments that allow leaders to understand their agile capabilities, along with the capabilities of their teams and even the organization overall. Such measurement provides leaders with the opportunity to make course corrections on an ongoing basis.

But all of that measurement truly comes from one foundation. Even though, for example, we use different assessments for leaders, teams and whole organizations, all of them use the five drivers of The Agile Model® as a foundation. This is a unique aspect of our approach, and it's important because it clarifies what we're talking about when we talk about agility.

In this manner, agility matters at the individual, team and organizational levels. The only aspect that changes is the nature of the environment and the goals. For example, the environment for an individual leader involves both the leader's critical tasks and the people around him or her through which work must get done. The environment for the team and organization is broader. For example, at the broadest level, the organizational environment for a large multinational corporation involves not only the organization's customers, suppliers and competitors. It also involves, though, geopolitical concerns across nations, risks posed by conflict and more.

The Agile Model®

The ability to anticipate change requires you to pay systematic attention to multiple contextual elements (both internal and external): the general environment, including economic, political, and cultural developments; specifics of your business, including technical issues and the dynamics of customer demands; and organizational factors, including strategy, finances, structure, and business practices. You must have effective processes for visioning, sensing, and monitoring.

The ability to generate confidence requires you to address issues related to how your people, internal and external to your organization, understand and feel about their capacities, and the dynamics involved with creating satisfaction for all of your organization's stakeholders. Personal awareness of strengths and developmental needs is the starting point for self-confidence and one's capability to generate confidence. Much of this rests squarely on your ability to inspire trust, commitment, communication, and involvement in all stakeholders—internally and externally—building the DNA of your culture and values through actions. You must have effective processes of connecting, aligning, and engaging.

The ability to initiate action requires you to assure that within your organization there is an inclination toward proactive action as well as the means to advance focused activity reasonably and promptly. You must have a shared mindset and effective processes for creating that bias for action and sense of urgency, for improving active and widespread decision-making, and for actively collaborating with internal and external stakeholders.

The ability to liberate thinking requires you to assure that your organization has the means to originate and incorporate new ideas. You must have effective processes that build capacity and energy for innovation, also creating that inclination towards, and bias for, innovation, focusing on customers to provide the fuel for innovation, and generating meaningful concept diversity from high levels of idea engagement with all stakeholders. This driver is essentially concerned with creating a supportive environment to build capacity and energy for innovation.

The ability to evaluate results requires you to align vision to action, acquiring the knowledge and facts necessary to learn from and improve the actions you and your organization take. You must have effective processes for creating expectations aligned to your success model, providing real-time feedback throughout the value chain and with your people, and identifying and utilizing fact-based measures that link each part of the organization to an overall success map. The after-action-review process is a best practice illustration from the military that is often missing in private-sector organizations.

Leadership Agility involves a host of behaviors that support 15 specific agile processes. We've categorized those into five drivers within The Agile Model® as listed below.

• **Anticipating Change:** Requires effective processes for *Visioning, Sensing and Monitoring*

• **Generating Confidence:** Requires effective processes for *Connecting, Aligning and Engaging*

• **Initiating Action:** Requires effective processes for *Bias for Action, Decision-Making Capability and Collaborating*

• **Liberating Thinking:** Requires effective processes for *Bias for Innovation, Focusing on Customers and Idea Diversity*

• **Evaluating Results:** Requires processes for *Creating Expectations, Real-Time Feedback and Fact-Based Measures*

It's important to note that we've always strongly believed that strength in all five of the drivers is important. That is, over-reliance on any one of them will result in less agility than a balanced strength across all five. For example, if a leader focuses entirely on Liberating Thinking but never Evaluates Results, innovation will likely be inefficient. Novel solutions may emerge, but will they be useful? Will they be directed toward what's needed by the organization? How do we know that they're working?

Similarly, if a leader or organization focuses entirely on Generating Confidence but never Initiates Action, goal accomplishment will likely suffer. Connecting, aligning and engaging one's team is critical, but without a spark to make progress, the team won't live up to expectations.

So, we wondered, is there a way to take a fresh look at the data and see whether all five drivers really matter? Could we tell quantitatively, using statistics, whether the drivers were different? And what might those findings tell us about the future of building agile capacity in leaders and organizations?

Our Research Questions

In thinking more about how we can continue to refine our knowledge of the science and practice of agility, we decided upon the following research questions, keeping in mind the nature of the data available for analysis. In particular, we wanted to know:

1. Do people tend to rate themselves equally in competence across the five drivers within The Agile Model®, or do they tend to be stronger on specific drivers than others?

2. Are there differences in how people in Western cultures rate themselves versus people in Asian cultures?

3. What can we learn from the highest and lowest rated 15 agile processes?

4. Is the way we're measuring the five drivers reliable? Are the five drivers related to each other yet distinct?

5. Do the five drivers relate to relevant outcome measures such as speed of decision making, creating employee engagement, creating customer satisfaction, managing change and sensing and responding to patterns and trends? If so, how? And are there drivers that seem to dominate the others in importance?

6. Being focused, fast and flexible is important for many reasons, but do organizations that exhibit these characteristics also have better financial performance?

Although our data aren't perfect—we couldn't for example, survey everyone within a specific organization or obtain ratings of their performance from others around them—the numbers we have on hand do allow us to shed considerable light on these questions.

Nicholas F. Horney, Ph.D. **67**

What the Data Say

At the level of the individual leader, the assessment we developed and have used with thousands of leaders is the Leadership Agility Profile™ (LAP). We've used the LAP™ to coach executives, to develop leaders in specific workshops, and to promote leadership agility within larger leadership development efforts.

In 2006, we developed a workshop titled "Strategic Agility and Resilience: Embracing Change to Drive Growth" for the American Management Association®. During the workshop, which also includes an in-depth exploration of The Agile Model® and how it relates to creating focused, fast and flexible leaders and organizations, participants review their LAP™ self-assessment results. The LAP™ measures all five drivers within The Agile Model® through a series of 75 items. We also include in this particular version of the assessment a handful of informative questions related to leadership agility and perceptions of the organization.

From these data, we analyzed a recent sample of responses from 1,078 leaders, of whom 579 were based in the United States and 499 were based in Japan. The leaders varied widely in industry (e.g., government, manufacturing, pharmaceuticals, health care, energy, etc.) and function (e.g., operations, sales, finance, research and development, human resources, etc.) and were relatively experienced leaders, with 65 percent reporting at least five years in a key leadership position.

YEARS IN KEY LEADERSHIP POSITION

LESS THAN 2 — 13%
2 TO 5 — 23%
5 TO 10 — 29%
10 TO 20 — 27%
MORE THAN 20 — 9%

Inside the LAP™

The 75 items in the LAP™ assess the behaviors associated with each of the five drivers within The Agile Model®: Anticipating Change, Generating Confidence, Initiating Action, Liberating Thinking and Evaluating Results. Each of the five drivers, however, comprises three sub-elements, or processes.

Leaders take the LAP™ through an online questionnaire-style assessment. Calculating the average score across specific groups of items allows us to determine a specific score for each of the 15 processes; calculating the average scores of these items within each of the five drivers reveals larger trends within the data.

Question 1: Do people tend to rate themselves equally in competence across the five drivers within The Agile Model®, or do they tend to be stronger on specific drivers than others?

At the driver level across all respondents in our sample, the average score for Anticipating Change was the lowest and the average score for Generating Confidence was the highest as displayed below from a scale of 1 (lowest) to 5 (highest).

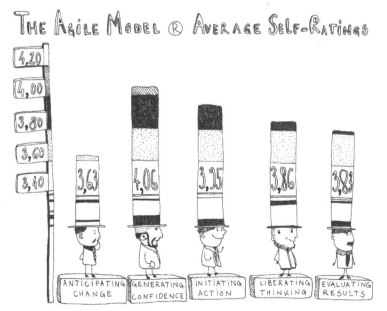

THE AGILE MODEL ® AVERAGE SELF-RATINGS

4,20
4,00
3,80
3,60
3,40

3,63 4,06 3,95 3,86 3,8

ANTICIPATING CHANGE | GENERATING CONFIDENCE | INITIATING ACTION | LIBERATING THINKING | EVALUATING RESULTS

Although self-ratings of agility did not differ in a meaningful way across leaders from specific functions or industries, we did find small but statistically significant positive correlations (.11 to .16, p < .001) between years in a key leadership position and ratings of the five drivers within The Agile Model®.

This means that those with more years of key leadership experience tended to rate their agility slightly higher than those with fewer years of key leadership experience.

Question 2: Are there differences in how people in Western cultures rate themselves versus people in Asian cultures?

Given that we had a conveniently cross-cultural sample, we wanted to see whether leaders in the United States tended to rate themselves differently than Japanese leaders. Across each driver, as displayed below, U.S.-based leaders' self-ratings were higher than Japanese leaders' self-ratings. All differences are statistically significant at the $p < .001$ level.

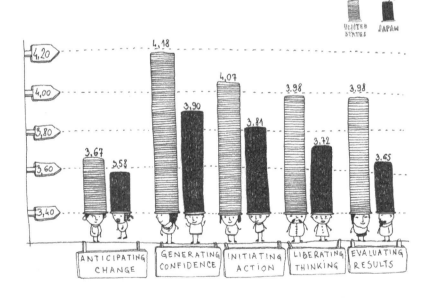

The Agile Model® Average Self-Ratings

What we find interesting is not necessarily that leaders from these two countries and cultures tended to rate themselves differently. What's interesting is that the trends are exactly the same: Regardless of country, leaders on average rated their abilities in Anticipating Change as the lowest, followed by Evaluating Results, Liberating Thinking, Initiating Action and Generating Confidence as the highest.

Such findings suggest a need for continued emphasis on certain areas of The Agile Model®--particularly Anticipating Change and Evaluating Results—in order to increase overall agility.

Question 3: What can we learn from the highest and lowest rated 15 agile processes?

Our findings regarding trends at the driver level are interesting; however, we wanted to dig deeper. In particular, are there particular agile processes among the 15 that people tend to rate as strengths and others they tend to rate as weaknesses?

As a reminder, the 15 agile processes are sub-components of the five drivers within The Agile Model®. Our analysis reported above showed that leaders rated their abilities in Anticipating Change lower than their abilities in the other drivers. But looking at the data in terms of individual processes could provide additional insight.

For example, we knew that Anticipating Change was at the bottom. But were all of its supporting processes—Visioning, Sensing, and Monitoring—also rated lower than the rest? What else might be part of the picture?

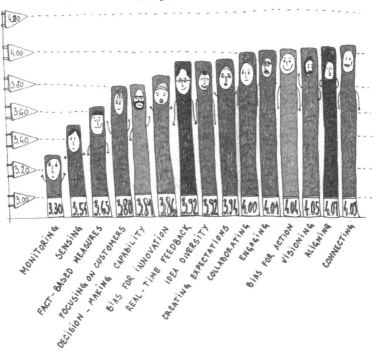

THE AGILE MODEL ® AVERAGE SELF-RATINGS OF THE 15 AGILE PROCESSES

3.30	3.54	3.65	3.80	3.84	3.86	3.92	3.92	3.94	4.00	4.01	4.04	4.05	4.01	4.01

MONITORING, SENSING, FACT-BASED MEASURES, FOCUSING ON CUSTOMERS, DECISION-MAKING CAPABILITY, BIAS FOR INNOVATION, REAL-TIME FEEDBACK, IDEA DIVERSITY, CREATING EXPECTATIONS, COLLABORATING, ENGAGING, BIAS FOR ACTION, VISIONING, ALIGNING, CONNECTING

As we expected and as displayed above, two processes from Anticipating Change—Monitoring and Sensing were the two lowest-rated processes. But rounding out the bottom five were Fact-Based Measures (a sub-component of Evaluating Results), Focusing on Customers (a sub-component of Liberating Thinking) and Decision-Making Capability (a sub-component of Initiating Action).

In fact, the remaining sub-component of Anticipating Change, Visioning, was actually among the top three processes, along Aligning and Connecting, which are both sub-components of Generating Confidence. The two remaining processes in the top five were Bias for Action (a sub-component of Initiating Action) and Engaging (the remaining sub-component of Generating Confidence).

VUCA Masters:
Developing Leadership Agility Fitness for the New World of Work

Question 4: Is the way we're measuring the five drivers reliable? Are the five drivers related to each other yet distinct?

Although we've previously established that our measurement tools are reliable, it's wise to continue monitoring the internal consistency of survey measures. In the type of measurement done in many surveys and assessments, the areas being measured are multifaceted. There are many behaviors, for example, that contribute to the overall driver of Anticipating Change.

THE AGILE MODEL® DRIVER RELIABILITIES

One of the most common ways to do this for assessments like the LAP™ is to calculate what's called the Cronbach's alpha coefficient. Outlining the theory and math behind that is beyond the scope of this work, but suffice it to say that low Cronbach's alpha coefficients (say, below .70) indicate that the assessment items aren't holding together well—the way in which people respond to them might suggest that the assessment isn't really measuring just one "thing." On the other hand, higher Cronbach's alpha coefficients suggest a higher level of precision in the measurement. Ideally, these statistics are high but not too high (for example, higher than .95). The reason one wouldn't want an alpha coefficient that's too high is that it would indicate unnecessary repetitiveness in the items.

For example, we could construct an assessment that asked you to "Indicate the extent to which you like chicken." If we asked you to respond to the exact same item 10 times in a row, you'd probably answer it the same way each time. The alpha coefficient in that instance would be 1.00.

As displayed, the drivers within The Agile Model® have ideal internal consistency in the data we analyzed from 1,078 leaders, as indicated by the Cronbach's alpha coefficients ranging from .87 to .93. This tells us that our measurement of the drivers is indeed reliable.

But calculating the Cronbach's alpha coefficient doesn't tell us anything about how the drivers relate to each other. For example, are they really all just measuring the same thing, or are they related-but-different? Our prior work and analyses suggest that they are indeed related-but-different, so we expected to find a similar result when examining these data.

One relatively simple way to do this is to simply look at the correlations among the drivers. If they're too close to 1.00, that would mean that they are redundant and not distinct. As displayed, the correlations among the different drivers confirm our hypothesis that they would be related but not identical. All correlations displayed are statistically significant at the $p < .001$ level. Therefore, we can conclude that the elements within The Agile Model® are certainly related to each other. But they're also not so strongly related to suggest redundancy.

	1	2	3	4	5
1. ANTICIPATING CHANGE	1.00				
2. GENERATING CONFIDENCE	0.63	1.00			
3. INITIATING ACTION	0.66	0.79	1.00		
4. LIBERATING THINKING	0.65	0.70	0.81	1.00	
5. EVALUATING RESULTS	0.65	0.76	0.76	0.71	1.00

Question 5: Do the five drivers relate to relevant outcome measures such as speed of decision making, creating employee engagement, creating customer satisfaction, managing change and sensing and responding to patterns and trends? If so, how? And are there drivers that seem to dominate the others in importance?

The analyses reported above reveal useful information about The Agile Model® and current trends among leaders, but these analyses don't address a critical question: Does one need all five drivers to be agile?

Fortunately, our data are such that we could investigate this more closely. In addition to the 75 items that comprise the LAP™, we asked participants to rate their abilities on a handful of specific behaviors and processes that we consider important outcomes of the behaviors described by The Agile Model®. Specifically, we asked for self-assessments of the following five outcome areas: (1) speed of decision making, (2) creating employee engagement, (3) creating customer satisfaction, (4) managing change and (5) sensing and responding to patterns and trends.

As we described above, years in a key leadership position correlated positively with ratings of the five drivers of The Agile Model®. Not surprisingly, years in a key leadership position also tended to correlate with ratings of the five outcome areas listed above. Therefore, we wanted to see if a relationship existed between the five drivers of The Agile Model® and the five outcome areas above and beyond any changes that could be attributed to years in a key leadership position.

Not to get overly complicated, but a specific statistical analysis technique (hierarchical regression) allowed us to do just that. It allowed us to tease out the relationship in a more nuanced, scientific way. And what we found was compelling.

Above and beyond any differences in leadership experience, the drivers within The Agile Model® positively relate with these key outcome areas. This provides evidence that the drivers matter, but more importantly, the results suggest that specific drivers may matter more for certain outcomes than for others. In particular:

• For <u>speed of decision making</u>: The five drivers within The Agile Model® together explained 21 percent of the variance above and beyond leadership experience, with Anticipating Change and Initiating Action being significant individual predictors of self-rated quicker decision making. **Interpretation: Anticipating Change and Initiating Action are likely key contributors to making decisions faster.**

• For <u>creating employee engagement</u>: The five drivers within The Agile Model® together explained 32 percent of the variance above and beyond leadership experience, with Generating Confidence, Initiating Action, Liberating Thinking, and Evaluating Results being significant individual predictors of self-rated higher ability in creating engagement. **Interpretation: If you want people who are better at creating employee engagement, Generating Confidence is where you'd want to start in The Agile Model®.**

• For <u>creating customer satisfaction</u>: The five drivers within The Agile Model® together explained 18 percent of the variance above and beyond leadership experience, with Initiating Action, Liberating Thinking, and Evaluating Results being significant individual predictors of self-rated higher ability in creating customer satisfaction. **Interpretation: Customer satisfaction demands a proactive, creative approach and incorporates measurement.**

• For <u>managing change</u>: The five drivers within The Agile Model® together explained 29 percent of the variance above and beyond leadership experience, with Anticipating Change, Initiating Action, and Liberating Thinking being significant individual predictors of self-rated higher ability in managing change. **Interpretation: Managing change requires a combination of imaginative preparation and bias for action.**

• For <u>sensing and responding to patterns and trends</u>: The five drivers within The Agile Model® together explained 32 percent of the variance above and beyond leadership experience, with Anticipating Change, Generating Confidence, Liberating Thinking, and Evaluating Results being significant individual predictors of higher ability in sensing and responding to patterns and trends. **Interpretation: Sensing and responding—key elements of the concept of agility by definition—is a complex process that requires multiple capabilities.**

These findings confirm what we've been finding through our work with executives and their organizations for years. Namely, becoming agile won't happen with a single approach. Instead, it's a coordinated, balanced approach that supports both the mindset and related behaviors required for agility.

Over-reliance on any one driver within The Agile Model® is an incorrect application of it and should be avoided. The musicians among us can think of The Agile Model® like chord, a set of notes that together create something richer, more fulfilling than any one of the parts on its own.

Question 6: Being focused, fast and flexible is important for many reasons, but do organizations that exhibit these characteristics also have better financial performance?

The Agile Model® is a recognized best practice and helpful leadership framework. It has helped thousands of leaders and teams unlock their agile potential.

But we were curious to look at whether our data might reveal any correlation between the outcome of agility—being focused, fast and flexible—and the firm's financial performance. Theoretically, we have strong arguments to suggest this link. We also have our own experience working with executives and organizations.

Still, we wanted to look deeper. Like any set of data, the one we analyzed here isn't perfect. And although our LAP™ is a validated instrument, it doesn't by itself produce the data to answer this question. For that, we turned to a handful of extra questions that we included in the assessments. We included three simple questions that asked each respondent to indicate the extent to which his or her organization is (1) focused, (2) fast and (3) flexible. In separate question, we asked each respondent to describe his or her company's current financial performance as compared to the past five years (e.g., worse, about the same, better, etc.).

Nicholas F. Horney, Ph.D.   77

We knew that in analyzing these data for a correlation between the ratings of being focused, fast and flexible and the estimates of financial performance the odds were stacked against us to find anything. We were asking only one member of the organization, which makes the validity of their answer depend upon their knowledge and perspective. We were also asking for an estimate of financial performance, which again depends upon their viewpoint. A precedent does exist, however, to use subjective measures of financial performance when other objective indicators are not available.

With these odds against us, we didn't expect to find anything. We thought that even if we found a small glimpse of a positive correlation between how people responded to these questions that we'd be thrilled. Undaunted, then, we analyzed the data.

It turns out that we did find a positive correlation—not just between, for example, being fast and firm performance—but between all three and firm performance. Likely due to the measurement issues described above, these correlations aren't huge. But they are statistically significant, and they are in the positive direction. We found a positive correlation between ratings of an organization being focused and ratings of firm performance (correlation of .18, $p < .001$), between ratings of an organization being fast and ratings of firm performance (correlation of .10, $p < .05$) and between ratings of an organization being flexible and ratings of firm performance (correlation of .12, $p < .01$).

Insights and Lessons

The data we analyzed from 1,078 leaders revealed a number of useful insights. The final sections that follow outline some of what we see as the key ways to interpret these findings as well as a list of action steps individual leaders, teams or organizations could find useful in building their own internal capacity to be agile in this turbulent world.

Interpreting the Findings

Anticipating Change is a competency ripe for growth. In looking simply at the average way in which leaders rated their competence across the five drivers within The Agile Model®, we found that Anticipating Change is clearly the biggest area for improvement. Furthermore, we found that two of the three processes that support Anticipating change—Monitoring and Sensing—were the two lowest-rated of the 15 processes overall. This suggests that leaders could use additional support in developing both of these areas, and that doing so would support their development as agile leaders.

The other three low-rated processes—Fact-Based Measures, Focusing on Customers, And Decision-Making Capability—also suggest areas of focus for today's leaders. Using fact-based measures, for example, requires an appreciation for the use of data to support decision making—suggesting that this area could be addressed in tandem with decision-making capability. Making decisions based upon data and fact-based measures also requires some technical ability combined with critical thinking skills.

These data also support the importance of focusing on customers, which we're noticing as an increasingly critical capability among our clients as they seek new avenues for differentiation in the marketplace.

U.S.-based leaders tend to rate themselves higher than Japanese leaders. We found significant differences between average self-ratings from U.S.-based leaders when compared with leaders in Japan. We didn't find this surprising. What's meaningful here is that the Japanese leaders' average ratings on the five drivers within The Agile Model® were in the exact same rank order as U.S. leaders' average ratings. This supports the notion that Anticipating Change is the driver about which leaders have the least confidence.

Measurement of the five drivers within The Agile Model® is solid. Examining the measurement statistics and response patterns across the 1,078 leaders revealed reassuring evidence for the instruments reliability. It's an internally consistent assessment, and each facet, although related the others, appears to be distinct.

The five drivers all matter for relevant outcomes. When we investigated how the five drivers within The Agile Model® related to relevant outcome measures such as speed of decision making, creating employee engagement, creating customer satisfaction, managing change and sensing and responding to patterns and trends, we did so using hierarchical multiple regression. That allowed us to hold constant the primary potentially confounding variable in our data—years of experience. Our findings suggest that each driver matters in relation to these outcomes, above and beyond the number of years the person served in a key leadership position.

None of the drivers dominated others in importance. This provides additional evidence for approaching The Agile Model® holistically. Over-relying on any one driver will not produce agility. All five need to be present, and organizations would be well-served by continuing to pay heed to this fact.

Focused, fast and flexible organizations are poised to benefit financially. Despite the odds stacked against us in terms of the limitations of the data we had available, we found positive, statistically significant correlations between the outcomes of being agile and organizational performance. We suspect that these results would be even stronger with enhanced measurement on both ends—more nuanced ratings of being focused, fast and flexible and more objective ratings of financial performance.

We're encouraged by these findings. They further validate The Agile Model® and help us better understand current trends among leaders, based upon what they told us directly through their responses to the LAP™.

Action Steps

So what are some of the actions you should consider based upon our most recent findings? Here are a few:

1. Measure agility. Clearly, being agile matters because it's the focused, fast and flexible leaders, teams and organizations that survive and thrive in this volatile, uncertain, complex and ambiguous (VUCA) world. Our Leadership Agility Profile™ (which produced the data we analyzed and reported here) measures the 75 behaviors, 15 processes and five drivers within The Agile Model®. Also based upon The Agile Model® are the Team Agility Profile™ and Organizational Agility Profile™, which allow leaders to assess agility at the level of the group or organization, respectively.

Beyond our instruments, your organization likely already has metrics that people track. Are they the right metrics? How do they connect to the focus, speed and flexibility of the organization? Measurement determines priorities, bringing the foggy nature of human behavior within organizations into focus.

2. Anticipate change. One of the most prominent aspects of what we found is that the driver of Anticipating Change clearly is an area that requires additional support and focus by leaders in order to become agile. Our Leadership Agility Development Guide™, for example, suggests a number of ways in which leaders can become better at anticipating change, along with suggestions within other agility domains.

For Monitoring and Sensing, it's critical to improve one's ability to use fact-based measures to detect changes in the environment. It's also important to build one's active listening skills because some of the best knowledge about what's going on both in your organization and outside its boundaries comes from your employees. They must feel as though they can share such knowledge, even if it's bad news. Such psychological safety goes a long way in creating an organization that notices and responds to weak signals of danger.

3. Reconsider what constitutes "leadership." Much of what we consider leadership comes from our experiences. We see what works and try to emulate it, we see what doesn't work and try not to do that. That's not necessarily a bad idea, but it doesn't help us when we face entirely new situations.

The VUCA world we face today consists of new situations on an increasingly frequent basis. Therefore, the practices that worked for leaders yesterday may not necessarily work for them tomorrow. Similarly, organizations need to have a healthy wariness of repeating history by simply doing what worked well somewhere else and hoping for the same results.

When we closely inspect the top 15 processes that support the five drivers within The Agile Model®, we find that the top five are, in order from high to low: Connecting, Aligning, Visioning, Bias for Action and Engaging. These are important, and there's nothing wrong with them at all. But they do align more closely with our traditional notions of leadership, particularly in terms of inspiring others and taking action. Again, there's nothing intrinsically wrong with these notions at all.

But by themselves, these processes aren't enough. They will not create agility. We suggest that leadership should continue to focus on these processes. But we would all be well-served to also focus on the less-popular but increasingly important processes of Monitoring, Sensing, Fact-Based Measures, Focusing on Customers, and Decision-Making Capability.

Conclusion

Since 2001, we've been working with leaders, teams and organizations to become more agile. Using data and science to support our work has always been important, and the analyses of data from 1,078 leaders reported here is one example. We hope that these findings provoke thought, conversation and action—continued progress in your agility journey.

Dr. Kozhi Sidney Makai – VUCA Master

(View a brief video on the VUCA Master story of Dr. Kozhi Sidney Makai -- (99+) VUCA Masters Series -- Dr. Kozhi Sidney Makai | LinkedIn).

Dr. Makai has demonstrated his ability to master the VUCA (volatility, uncertainty, complexity, and ambiguity) experienced in business and in his personal life. He is the founder of Kozhi Makai Worldwide, a strengths-based idea studio focused on aligning professional and personal goals to generate sustainable performance. With more than 19 years of experience in human and organizational behavior, Kozhi partners with companies, organizations and individuals with the desire to thrive and become more effective leaders using both practical and research-based tools to lead and advise clients.

He earned his Bachelor's in Speech Communication in three and a half years from Sam Houston State University, his Master's in Leadership and Influence in eight months from Jones International University, and his Ph.D. in Applied Management and Decision Sciences in 18 months from Walden University. Dr. Makai is a Senior Professional in Human Resources® and Certified Professional in Learning and Performance®. And because that simply wasn't enough, Kozhi also just completed his second doctoral degree, a Doctorate of Psychology, with a focus on Positive Performance Psychology.

He lives out his motto of bringing others From Potential to Performance® through his simple mission – to use behavioral science to help others thrive, both in and outside of the workplace. I created a brief video about why Kozhi represents all of the characteristics of a VUCA Master in both his business and personal life. Kozhi Sidney Makai VUCA Master - YouTube

Leadership Agility Fitness Levels and Types

Leadership Agility Fitness

Leadership Agility Fitness focuses on one key element of the Domains of Business Agility – the human element of Leadership Agility Fitness. Levels of Leadership Agility Fitness are represented by the combination of Drivers of The AGILE Model®. The aggregate of an organization's Leadership Fitness is one of the major factors in predicting its Business Agility Maturity. "Continuing from last year, the data highlights that leadership style remains the biggest challenge to business agility adoption faced by most organizations. Related to leadership style, the analysis revealed the challenges of a lack of vision as well as insufficient sponsorship for business agility by management. Experience, as well as earlier studies, suggest that with the right mindset and associated organizational support, a leader sets the tone for the entire organization. In some respondent organizations, leaders continue to use leadership styles and behaviors that are consistent with the legacy culture, and not the new culture that the organization is trying to instill. This sends a mixed message to the rest of the organization. " (BAI, Business Agility Report, 2020) A key recommendation for leaders is "Be mindful of your leadership style. From day one of your business agility journey, strive to model the new leadership styles and behaviors that are consistent with your organization's goals for transformation. How you show up as a leader will be noticed and will often be emulated by your workforce." (BAI, Business Agility Report, 2020) Over the past 20 years of Leadership and Organizational Agility research, consulting, writing, etc., it has been important to capture Leadership Agility Fitness baseline measures and repeat this assessment at least annually as you would do with an annual physical.

Leadership Agility Fitness is a framework that encourages true balance of the 5 key drivers found in The AGILE Model®, with respect to a rapidly changing VUCA environment. The amount, volume, velocity, intensity, etc. of "noise" we encounter with change requires us to become more agile. And the secret to becoming more agile as a Leader is to demonstrate that you can be focused, fast and flexible, even in the worst circumstances. The AGILE Model® offers the framework that will enable you to identify your Leadership Agility Fitness Level (AFL) and help identify a plan to help you attain and sustain the highest leadership agility fitness level you are willing to achieve. But it takes work, just like it takes work to achieve your personal physical fitness goal.

AGILITY FITNESS™

Section 3: Leadership Agility Profile™: 360 Assessment Results

This is your summary chart for the LEADERSHIP AGILITY PROFILE™. You can view how you rated yourself compared to how your team rated you in each of the key leadership agility behaviors. You can identify the areas requiring the most immediate attention as well as those areas where you have demonstrated strengths. Successful leaders are able to build from their strengths and find sustainable ways to improve where needed.

J. SAMPLE							Total Score	
	Self	All	Self	All	Self	All	Self	All
Anticipate Change	Visioning		Sensing		Monitoring			
	4.00	3.78	4.40	4.20	4.40	4.22	4.27	4.07
Generating Confidence	Connecting		Aligning		Engaging			
	3.20	3.89	2.40	3.75	2.80	3.94	2.80	3.86
Initiating Action	Bias for Action		Decision Making		Collaborating			
	4.40	3.55	4.60	4.05	4.20	3.83	4.40	3.81
Liberating Thinking	Innovation		Customer Focus		Idea Diversity			
	2.60	3.74	3.60	3.89	3.40	3.94	3.20	3.86
Evaluating Results	Creating Expectations		Real-Time Feedback		Fact-Based Measures			
	3.80	3.48	3.60	3.48	4.40	3.54	3.93	3.50
Overall Leadership Agility Index™							3.72	3.82

VUCA Masters:
Developing Leadership Agility Fitness for the New World of Work

Physical fitness is the body's ability to function efficiently and effectively. It is a state of being that consists of at least five health-related and six skill-related, physical fitness components, each of which contributes to total quality of life. Physical fitness is associated with a person's ability to work effectively, enjoy leisure time, be healthy, resist hypokinetic diseases, and meet emergency situations. It is related to, but different from, health and wellness. Although the development of physical fitness is the result of many things, optimal physical fitness is not possible without regular physical activity.

The five components of health-related physical fitness are body composition, cardiovascular fitness, flexibility, muscular endurance, and strength. Each health related fitness characteristic has a direct relationship to good health and reduced risk of hypokinetic disease.

Possessing a moderate amount of each component of health-related fitness is essential to disease prevention and health promotion, but it is not essential to have exceptionally high levels of fitness to achieve health benefits. High levels of health-related fitness relate more to performance than health benefits. For example, moderate amounts of strength are necessary to prevent back and posture problems, whereas high levels of strength contribute most to improved performance in activities such as football and jobs involving heavy lifting.

Before starting any new exercise program to increase your fitness, think of the pre-workout physical necessary before you go to the gym or engage a trainer (coach) to help you develop a personalized fitness program. Your fitness program will depend on many factors, some readily visible such as your current state of fitness, other factors require digging a little deeper – like drawing blood for a cholesterol level, you will need to seek information about your "body chemistries" that are not in your direct line of sight. Fitness, whether physical or organizational, is a life-long commitment, not an annual strategic planning retreat, or one time training event.

So let's begin by reviewing your Leadership Agility Profile (self-assessment or 360) which if based on The AGILE Model®. The results of the LAP assessment serve as the "pre-workout physical" for your Leadership Agility Fitness Plan. We all know that no one measure (e.g. weight, heartrate, cholesterol level, blood pressure, etc.) from a physical will provide you a comprehensive view of your physical fitness. It takes multiple tests that are interpreted with the aid of a trained physician and perhaps personal trainer to help you create your fitness plan. As with the physical exam, the LAP provides 75 individual measures of your Leadership Agility Fitness that are combined into 5 key drivers of Leadership Agility. These key drivers can be interpreted independently to help you improve individual aspects of Leadership Agility, like the ability to Generate Confidence. However, the concept of Leadership Agility Fitness Levels (AFL) is based on a combination of these 5 Drivers, like you would receive during your physical exam. When distributed in a table, there are 6 AFL Levels. The lowest AFL is Level 0 (none of the 5 Leadership Agility Drivers from the results of the LAP reflects a strength). The highest Leadership AFL is Level 5 (all of the 5 Leadership Agility Drivers from the results of the LAP reflect strengths). Within each of the Leadership AFLs are AFL Types that are based on the combinations of the agility drivers from The AGILE Model®. Agility Fitness Levels (AFL) codes -- Could be AFL-O (FRAGILE); AFL-1A, AFL-1G, AFL-1I, AFL-1L; AFL-1E; AFL-2AG, AFL-2AI, AFL-2AL, AFL-2AE, ...AFL-5 AGILE. A table illustrating Leadership AFLs and AFL Types is illustrated below:

Leadership Agility Fitness Levels

Level 5: VUCA Masters – All 5 Drivers are strong	Example -- AC, GC, IA, LT, ER
Level 4: Combination of 4 Strong Drivers	Example – AC, GC, IA, LT, ER
Level 3: Combination of 3 Strong Drivers	Example – AC, GC, IA, LT, ER
Level 2: Combination of 2 Strong Drivers	Example – AC, GC, IA, LT, ER
Level 1: Single Driver is strong	Example – AC, GC, IA, LT, ER
Level 0: Fragile Leaders – No strengths in any of the 5 Drivers	Example – AC, GC, IA, LT, ER

AC – Anticipate Change; GC – Generate Confidence; IA – Initiate Action; LT – Liberate Thinking; ER – Evaluate Results

FRAGILE = often exhibit behavior that reflects inappropriate behavior in VUCA situations (totally unaware of changes in people, processes or technology; do not display personal confidence nor encourage others to be confident; follows and defers to others for action and does not demonstrate a sense of urgency; offers bureaucratic solutions to problems and initiatives and does not create an environment of out-of-the-box thinking; operates mostly from gut feel without careful data gathering and analysis).

Agility Fitness Levels (AFL) are identified by the number of Drivers of The AGILE Model that are identified as strengths through a rigorous individual assessment process using the LAP or LAP 360. The continuum of AFL ranges from 0, where none of the 5 Drivers are identified as strengths to 5, where all 5 Drivers are identified as strengths. Therefore, the continuum anchors would reflect FRAGILE (0) to AGILE (5).

Types of Leadership Agility reflect the number and combinations of the Drivers indicated as strengths.

For example, AFL 1 Types would include the following behaviors:

AFL 1 1 Strong Driver with 5 Types	AGILE = Scout	AGILE = Generator	AGILE = Sprinter	AGILE = Liberator	AGILE = Evaluator
	Anticipate Change, Suppress Confidence, Resist Action, Bureaucratic, Measurement Averse	Unaware of changes, Generate confidence, Resist Action, Bureaucratic, Meas. Averse	Unaware of changes, Suppress Confidence, Initiate Action, Bureaucratic, Measurement Averse	Unaware of changes, Suppress confidence, Resist Action, Liberate thinking, Measurement Averse	Unaware of Changes, Suppress Confidence, Resist Action, Bureaucratic, Evaluate Results

AFL 1 Type A (Scout) – Strength is in Anticipating Change. This person has exceptional skills at forecasting things around the corner that are not clearly visible or apparent to others. He/she does this through constantly identifying and making sense of trends and patterns. Look to this person to be asking the "what-if" questions and applying scenario thinking. This person is keenly aware of trends, focuses on what's around the corner and what the future may

bring. The Scout uses techniques such as trend analysis, pattern analysis, scenario planning, etc. to determine signal strength of the changes that will likely impact people, processes and technology. He/she is likely to focus on the future as an independent activity without building confidence in others about what lies ahead. Often, this person believes that knowledge of the future (foresight) is enough without insight which can be used to build confidence in others. This person will leave the actions needed from this foresight up to others to take action and measure results of the actions taken. Very little emphasis is given by this person to others' ideas or inputs since this is perceived to be an independent activity and hence does not create an environment of liberated thinking.

AFL 1 Type G (Generator) – Strength is in Generating Confidence. This is the person who exhibits exceptional self confidence that is demonstrated in ways that are contagious for others. He/she becomes the power source for creating confidence with stakeholders regarding the actions being taken to address change. In engineering, a generator works by moving electrical conductors through a magnetic field. If your generator doesn't have magnets, it won't produce electricity. The magnetic field is created by taking some of the generator output voltage, converting it to DC, and feeding it to a coil to make an electromagnet. The same is true of a person who Generates Confidence. This person might be thought of as a "Generator" to create commitment to a concept, direction or idea. They keep people working happily together, often in subtle ways. However, this person does little to anticipate changes in the environment and is often surprised by changes that impact people, processes and technology. When the changes do occur, expect this person to be one of the first to bounce back and attempt to build confidence with and through others. This person is very much a team player, but does little to initiate actions or encourage others to think creatively. This person over-emphasizes the confidence-building activities over processes to evaluate whether actions being taken are having their desired impact.

Generators are attuned to people's feelings, and they like to talk about people but not in an aggressive way. People naturally turn to them for comfort in times of trouble. They speak warmly and lovingly to other people, who in turn speak warmly and lovingly of them. Generators may not be decisive or daring, but they keep people working happily together, often in subtle ways. They're focused on the group's well-being; one of the Generator's trademarks is being a team player. At lunch or at a company picnic, you'll see the Generators sitting together talking quietly— or not talking at all. Generators aren't trailblazers. In social situations, they'll rarely say anything inflammatory or unconventional. Generators prefer to fit in, not stand out. They seek to avoid conflict. Because they like to please other people, they'll say "yes" to something even though it would be better all around if they declined. As a result, Generators can take on too much and feel overwhelmed. In short, Generators are quiet, caring people who words express pride in the accomplishments of the team. Without them, the world would be a far less caring place.

 AFL 1 Type I (Sprinter) – Strength is in Initiating Action. When something needs to get done, this person has often already begun the task. "Make it happen, time's a wasting or just do it" would be phrases you would often hear from this person. Imagine someone who likes to get things done—whether it's building a new product or starting a new company. This person is a Sprinter. The Sprinter talks about actions. They don't have much time for small talk, or social niceties. In fact, they can be a little uncomfortable around people. They're quick to make decisions, quick to assign tasks, always on the move. Sprinters tend to focus on doing, not listening. They don't tell long stories or inquire into the health of your children. But they do talk about goals, about getting a jump on the competition, about the importance of getting the job done. Because Sprinters focus on getting things done, not on people, they can at times appear insensitive—even intimidating.

AFL 1 Type L (Liberator) – Strength is in Liberating Thinking. The environment created by this person encourages out-of-the-box thinking. In fact, he/she would ensure that there are opportunities for small tests so that you could fail faster and learn faster from the failure while celebrating the successes. Liberators are creative, always trying to find new ways to do things. They're willing to take chances, especially if their creative reputation

is on the line. They're fun to invite to a brainstorming meeting—they're always coming up with an out-of-the-box idea. Yet they can also be disorganized and lack follow-through. Liberators have a hard time focusing on one topic and listening. They lack a long attention span for something that doesn't involve or interest them. This can be frustrating for the people around them.

AFL 1 Type E (Evaluator) – Strength is in Evaluating Results. This person is metrics-driven and uses a host of resources to measure progress on projects, key initiatives, strategy, etc. You might often hear this person ask, "If you can't measure it, why waste time doing it?" Evaluators are focused on getting things done right. Their exacting sense of detail drives them to ask lots of questions. If an Evaluator is considering buying a new computer system, for example, she'll ask for all the comparative data. She'll make sure she has all her facts exactly in order. She'll make a list of the features she wants (the list is a trademark of the Evaluator). Often she'll postpone making a decision until she's certain she's got every piece of information she can find. Evaluators can seem tedious at times. But details are not tedious to the Evaluator. All those questions are crucial to getting the job done right. And their attention to detail can make Evaluators very valuable to have around. As you might surmise, Evaluators tend to be very cautious. They play out scenarios in great detail in their minds. They like to discuss these details with others, to make sure they've considered every angle. Evaluators tend to underestimate the amount of time they need to complete a project. Evaluators will give themselves "extensions" in order to make sure the project is done correctly the first time.

 AFL 2 Type IL (Sprinter/Liberator) -- Unaware of changes, Suppress confidence, Initiate action, Liberate thinking, Measurement averse

  AFL 2 Type LE (Liberator/Evaluator) -- Unaware of changes, Suppress confidence, Resist action, Liberate thinking, Evaluate results

  AFL 2 Type IE (Sprinter/Evaluator) -- Unaware of changes, Suppress confidence, Initiate action, Bureaucratic, Evaluate results

  AFL 2 Type GI (Generator/Sprinter) -- Unaware of changes, Generate confidence, Initiate action, Bureaucratic, Measurement averse

  AFL 2 Type GE (Generator/Evaluator) -- Unaware of changes, Generate confidence, Resist action, Bureaucratic, Evaluate results

  AFL 2 Type AE (Scout/Evaluator) -- Anticipate change, Suppress confidence, Resist action, Bureaucratic, Evaluate results

AFL 2 Type GL (Generator/Liberator) -- Unaware of changes, Generate confidence, Resist action, Liberate thinking, Measurement averse

  AFL 2 Type AG (Scout/Generator) -- Anticipate change, Generate confidence, Resist action, Bureaucratic, Measurement averse

  AFL 2 Type AI (Scout/Sprinter) -- Anticipate change, Suppress confidence, Initiate action, Bureaucratic, Measurement averse

  AFL 2 Type AL (Scout/Liberator) -- Anticipate change, Suppress confidence, Resist action, Liberate thinking, Measurement averse

I have provided descriptions of two illustrative Driver combinations below.

AFL Level 2 Type AG reflects combined strengths of Anticipating Change and Generating Confidence. He/she is a person especially strong at anticipating change while collaborating with others. This person generates confidence in others by empowering them with tools and techniques for sensing and monitoring trends with customers, suppliers and partners. It is this combination of self-confidence and anticipation of change which encourages confidence in others and his/her ability to provide foresight to others about impending changes makes this person a key team member or leader in a highly turbulent environment characterized by continuous change. Less emphasis is given by this person to initiating action resulting from the changes or encouraging others to think outside the box. He/she may also rely on others to evaluate whether actions taken to address change have had the desired impact.

AFL Level 2 Type IL reflects combined strengths of Initiating Action and Liberating Thinking. This person creates an environment for innovation so that new ideas can be quickly implemented. Speed of new idea generation is a driving force for this person. Little emphasis is placed on anticipating the changes that may be lurking in the environment and therefore may focus on new ideas for the current environment versus the new ideas needed for the changes creating a new or different environment. Little time is spent evaluating whether these new ideas have been fast enough or had their desired impact.

Similar combinations of Drivers would be reflected for AFL 3, AFL 4 and AFL 5 (VUCA Master) types.

Leadership Agility Narcosis

My experience in Navy Special Operations made me aware of nitrogen narcosis, a reversible alteration in consciousness producing a state similar to alcohol intoxication in divers at depth. It occurs to some small extent at any depth, but in most cases doesn't become noticeable until deeper diving depths, usually starting around 30 to 40 meters.

Due to its perception-altering effects, the onset of nitrogen narcosis may be hard to recognize, its severity is unpredictable, and in scuba diving, the resulting illogical behavior can be fatal. However, the cure for nitrogen narcosis is a simple one, as effects disappear within minutes upon ascending to shallower depths.

In diving, dangerous characteristics of nitrogen narcosis include the loss of decision-making ability, loss of focus, or impaired judgment. In the more extreme cases, some divers demonstrate a sense of invulnerability, extreme anxiety, exhilaration, giddiness, depression or even paranoia.

Regardless of the term used to describe the current and future marketplace (e.g., VUCA, turbulence, unrelenting change, organizational compression, etc.) the fact is that the world around us is accelerating at an alarming pace. Without a focused effort on the identification of strengths and weaknesses followed by targeted and often preemptive developmental activities, some leaders will likely show signs and symptoms similar to nitrogen narcosis that I refer to as **Leadership Agility Narcosis**™. A focused effort to develop your Leadership Agility Fitness will prevent Leadership Agility Narcosis™

When distributed in a table, there are 6 Agility Fitness Levels. The lowest Leadership AFL is Level 0 (none of the 5 Leadership Agility Drivers from the results of the LAP reflects a strength). The highest Leadership AFL is Level 5 (all of the 5 Leadership Agility Drivers from the results of the LAP reflect strengths). Within each of the Leadership AFLs are AFL Types that are based on the combinations of the agility drivers from The AGILE Model®. Agility Fitness Levels (AFL) codes -- Could be AFL-O (FRAGILE); AFL-1A, AFL-1G, AFL-1I, AFL-1L; AFL-1E; AFL-2AG, AFL-2AI, AFL-2AL, AFL-2AE, ...AFL-5 AGILE. A table reflecting all of the Leadership AFLs and AFL Types is illustrated below:

AGILE Level 5	All 5 Drivers are Strong Anticipate Change, Generate Confidence, Initiate Action, Liberate Thinking, Evaluate Results								
Level 4 4 Strong Drivers Combine for 5 Types	AGILE Unaware of changes, Generate confidence, Initiate Action, Liberate Thinking, Evaluate Results	AGILE Anticipate change, Suppress Confidence, Initiate action, Liberate Thinking Evaluate Results	AGILE Anticipate Change, Generate Confidence, Resist Action, Liberate Thinking, Evaluate Results	AGILE Anticipate Change, Generate Confidence, Initiate Action, Bureaucratic, Evaluate Results	AGILE Anticipate Change Generate Confidence Initiate Action, Liberate Thinking, Measurement Averse					
Level 3 3 Strong Drivers Combine for 10 Types	AGILE Unaware of changes, confidence, Liberate thinking, Evaluate results	AGILE Unaware of changes, Generate Confidence, Resist Acting, Liberate Thinking Evaluate Results	AGILE Unaware of changes, Generate Confidence, Initiate Action, Bureaucratic Evaluate Results	AGILE Unaware of changes, Initiate Action, Liberate Thinking, Measurement Averse	AGILE Anticipate change Suppress Confidence Initiate action, Bureaucratic, Evaluate Results	AGILE Anticipate Change, Suppress Confidence, Initiate action Liberate thinking, Measurement Averse	AGILE Anticipate Change, Generate Confidence Resist Action, Liberate Thinking, Measurement Averse	AGILE Anticipate change, Generate Confidence, Resist Action, Bureaucratic, Evaluate Results	AGILE Anticipate change, Generate Confidence, Initiate Action, Measurement Averse	AGILE Anticipate change, Suppress confidence, Resist action, thinking, Evaluate Results
Level 2 2 Strong Drivers Combine for 10 Types	AGILE Unaware of changes, Suppress Confidence, Initiate Action, Liberate Thinking, Measurement Averse	AGILE Unaware of changes, Suppress confidence, Resist Action, Liberate thinking, Evaluate results	AGILE Unaware of Changes, Suppress Confidence, Initiate Action, Bureaucratic Evaluate Results	AGILE Unaware of changes, Generate Confidence, Initiate Action, Bureaucratic, Meas. Averse	AGILE Unaware of Changes, Generate Confidence, Resist Action, Bureaucratic, Evaluate Results	AGILE Anticipate Change, Suppress Confidence, Resist Action, Bureaucratic, Evaluate Results	AGILE Unaware of Changes, Generate Confidence, Resist Action, Liberate Thinking Measurement Averse	AGILE Anticipate change, Generate Confidence, Resist Action, Bureaucratic, Measurement Averse	AGILE Anticipate Change, Suppress Confidence, Initiate Action, Bureaucratic, Measurement Averse	AGILE Anticipate change, Suppress confidence, Liberate thinking, Measurement Averse
Level 1 1 Strong Driver with 5 Types	AGILE = Scout Anticipate Change Suppress Confidence, Bureaucratic, Measurement Averse	AGILE = Encourager Unaware of changes, Generate confidence, Resist Action, Bureaucratic, Meas. Averse	AGILE = Sprinter Unaware of changes, Suppress Confidence, Initiate Action, Bureaucratic Measurement Averse	AGILE = Liberator Unaware of changes, Suppress confidence, Resist Action, Liberate thinking, Measurement Averse	AGILE = Evaluator Unaware of Changes Suppress Confidence, Resist Action, Bureaucratic, Evaluate Results					
FRAGILE Level 0	No Strong Drivers Unaware of Changes, Suppress Confidence, Resist Action, Bureaucratic, Measurement Averse								

References

2018 Hallenbeck, G., Horney, N. and Bateman, S. "Redefining Talent for the New World of Work: Stay Ahead of Change with Talent Portfolio Agility," Center for Creative Leadership & Agility Consulting Whitepaper.

2016 Horney, N., "The Gig Economy: A Disruptor Requiring HR Agility," HR People & Strategy, 39 (3), Summer 2016.

2015 Horney, N. and O'Shea, T. Focused, Fast & Flexible: Creating Agility Advantage in a VUCA World, Indie Books International

Nicholas F. Horney, Ph.D.   101

Lina Taylor – VUCA Master

"When life doesn't hand you the opportunities ..... create them. I believe in transforming our circumstances to achieve the extraordinary in business and in life."

Growing up in communist Bulgaria, Lina quickly realized that she had a choice: be defined by the system, the people, and the circumstances around her or step into the unknown and create her own path.

She is a two-time Olympian in beach volleyball, real estate business owner, mentor to elite athletes, co-founder of a college football award, wife of a Super Bowl champion, and a mother of three. Her life is full of reinventions and transformations, which didn't happen by accident.

At the age of 17, she figured out a way to come to the United States and get a higher education, paving the way for hundreds of other young people to similarly transform their lives.

After finishing college, Lina's drive and high aspirations were quickly getting drowned by the "Is it Friday yet?" culture at her first corporate job, so she set out to master the world of high performance and design a life of purpose and meaning. As she watched beach volleyball in the Olympics on TV, she decided to learn how to play the new, challenging sport and in two short years, overcoming big obstacles, she went from being a "weekend warrior" to an Olympian.

Just like in sports, Lina reinvented her career, translating her elite athletic skills into practical and effective business principles the she now shares with ambitious professionals and organizations from all over the world. Leading companies like Google, Twitter, M12 - the Microsoft Venture Fund, Intel, and Airbnb improve corporate culture, create employee engagement, and draw inspiration from Lina's story of resilience, determination, and grit.

Quick Leadership Agility Fitness Self-Assessment (A-15) – Provides more in-depth assessment of leadership agility than the Leadership Agility Snapshot that you completed earlier.

A-15™ Assessment

The A-15™ is a self-assessment and feedback tool designed from The Agile Model® and the 75 key leadership behaviors for creating and sustaining Agile organizations. This instrument focuses on the 15 sub-drivers and provides an quick self-assessment and discussion tool for use in Agility workshops. Read through each statement and rate yourself using the scale below and being as objective as possible. Total each sub-driver score and the total score in the box below and be prepared to discuss a couple of strength areas and a couple of areas needing some development.

Anticipating Change	1.	**Visioning:** Creating a clear mental picture of what the future could and should be along with the conviction to communicate and engineer that vision into everyday activities for self and team.	
	2.	**Sensing:** Recognizing the relatedness and patterns underlying information in various forms and from various sources; draws inferences or conclusions about the meaning of diverse information for the issue at hand.	
	3.	**Monitoring:** Identifying, collecting, organizing, and documenting data and information in ways that make the information most useful for subsequent assessment, analysis, and investigation.	
Generating Confidence	4.	**Connecting:** Influencing self and others within the organization to be excited, enthused, and committed to furthering the organization's objectives and for how their job roles connect to creating success.	
	5.	**Aligning:** Ensuring the right balance of resources, energy and priorities to achieve successful solutions and results in dynamic situations.	
	6.	**Engaging:** Building heightened emotional connection to the organization by influencing stakeholders to exert greater discretionary effort to the success of the organization.	
Initiating Action	7.	**Bias for Action:** Exhibiting initiative, energy and foresight in evaluating and responding to challenging situations, problems and opportunities.	
	8.	**Decision-Making:** Committing to a timely course of action which considers alternatives, risks and consequences in light of organizational goals, values, resources and constraints while encouraging same from team members.	
	9.	**Collaboration:** Moving quickly to find common ground for solutions among diverse interests; actively involves people inside and outside the immediate area creating conditions for cooperation.	
Liberating Thinking	10.	**Bias for Innovation:** Generating fresh, original or unconventional perspectives and approaches. Reexamines established ways of doing things with a thirst for real continuous improvement.	
	11.	**Customer Focus:** Developing solutions in a manner that demonstrates an understanding of internal and external customers' needs and desire for timely, cost-effective and value-added services.	
	12.	**Idea Diversity:** Seeking a variety of perspectives in an open-minded manner from traditional and nontraditional sources; seeks alternative, new or nontraditional approaches.	
Evaluating Results	13.	**Creating Expectations:** Clearly defining customer driven expected outcomes for self and all team members to create a good understanding to guide performance and achieve desired results.	
	14.	**Real-Time Feedback:** Identifying what needs to be done and proactively taking appropriate action; regularly communicating important feedback to team members and customers in timely manner	
	15.	**Fact-Based Measures:** Using data and information in a clear, rational and thorough process to assess and understand issues, evaluating options, forming accurate conclusions, and making decisions.	
		A-15™ Total Score	
		1 = need much improvement; 2 = need improvement; 3 = competent; 4 = strength area; 5 = major strength area	

Leadership Agility Fitness
in the
New World of Work

Work Design – Hybrid Work (references – WEF, IBM, Microsoft, Deloitte, McKinsey, John Boudreau) – implications for leadership agility at an individual and strategic lens.

In 2019, very few company leaders expected much impact to their business as a result of Covid-19. However, in 2020, all organizations across the globe were dramatically challenged by the health and business turbulence created by the Covid-19 Pandemic. In order to survive, most companies were forced to put in place a combination of virtual and in-person work design.

It appears that some form of hybrid work is here to stay as companies plan for post-Covid 19 work design. One of the more comprehensive global studies on hybrid work design was released by Microsoft in March 2021. "The year 2020 changed work forever, impacting every person and organization across the globe. Now, with widespread vaccinations in sight, we're on the brink of a disruption as great as last year's sudden shift to remote work: the move to hybrid — a blended model where some employees return to the workplace and others continue to work from home. We know two things for sure:

flexible work is here to stay, and the talent landscape has fundamentally shifted. With over 40 percent of the global workforce considering leaving their employer this year, a thoughtful approach to hybrid work is critical for leaders looking to attract and retain diverse talent. To help organizations through the transition, the 2021 Work Trend Index outlines findings from a study of more than 30,000 people in 31 countries." (Microsoft, 2021 Work Trend Index: Annual Report, "The Next Great Disruption is Hybrid Work – Are You Ready?," March 22, 2021)

Hybrid work is inevitable
Business leaders are on the brink of major changes to accommodate what employees want: the best of both worlds.

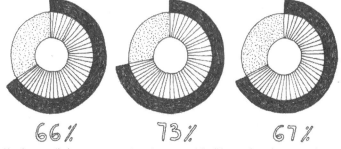

66%	73%	67%
of leaders say their company is considering redesigning office space for hybrid work	of employees want flexible remote work options to stay	of employees want more in-person work or collaboration post-pandemic

The Work Trend Index survey was conducted by an independent research firm, Edelman Data x Intelligence, among 31,092 full-time employed or self-employed workers across 31 markets between January 12, 2012 and January 25, 2021.

Microsoft 2012 Work Trend Index

Microsoft's CEO, Satya Nadella, emphasized the impact of Covid-19 on the way work is conducted now and into the future. "Over the past year, no area has undergone more rapid transformation than the way we work. Employee expectations are changing, and we will need to define productivity much more broadly — inclusive of collaboration, learning, and wellbeing to drive career advancement for every worker, including frontline and knowledge workers, as well as for new graduates and those who are in the workforce today. All this needs to be done with flexibility in when, where, and how people work."

The impact of the New World of Work, primarily defined by work design (e.g., hybrid work) will have significant impact on the readiness of leaders at all levels to demonstrate their leadership agility fitness.

Today's leaders are now strapped into a world in which the need for comparable transformation in the leadership of organizations is an absolute necessity to match the level of change happening in competitive, consumer, customer, and workforce environments. Leaders that demonstrate agility fitness will be skillful guides able to convert the external negative energy into positive internal energy coursing down through the organization creating confidence and success by becoming more focused, fast and flexible.

Implications for Leadership Agility for CHROs in the New World of Work

The upheavals in the business landscape brought about by Covid-19 will require CHROs who can help leaders in their organization become more agile in working with a broader talent portfolio in a hybrid work design. CHROs working with their business partners must be able to identify vital skills to survive and thrive in a VUCA world and identify the source of talent for those skills, whether full-time employees or contingent workers. Leadership Development and executive coaching programs will need to emphasize the new challenges of leading in a Hybrid Work environment. It is more difficult to lead a talent portfolio working in a hybrid design composed of a coalition of employees, contractors, contingent workers and consultants than it is to lead a team of people who work in-person at the organization's facility.

Nicholas F. Horney, Ph.D.

STEPS for a CHRO to develop his/her Leadership AGILITY FITNESS

The volume, velocity and intensity of the VUCA encountered from Covid-19 requires CHROs to demonstrate agility in HR policies, processes and practices to enable the organization to transform to a Hybrid Work design. The AGILE Model® offers the framework that will help CHROs attain and sustain their HR agility fitness targets as well as serve as an Agility Fitness Coach for others in the organization (Horney, Eckenrod, McKinney & Prescott, 2014). But it takes work to achieve this agility, just like it takes work to achieve your personal physical fitness goal. The following steps provide recommendations and illustrations to guide a CHRO.

Step 1. Anticipate change resulting from the Covid-19 by conducting an HR Agility Process Audit – Implications for HR processes (e.g., job analysis, recruiting, onboarding, performance management, talent assessment, etc.). Example – Modify Job Analysis Process to Work Analysis -- HR will need to shift its reliance on job analysis to implement work analysis focused on the tasks involved in accomplishing the work, regardless of whether the worker is a full-time employee or a contingent worker. HR should consult with its internal client functions to determine what work is best accomplished in-person or virtually and by full-time employees, contingent workers, contractors, etc.

Agility Drivers	Key Agile Processes (Illustrations)	From Job Analysis to Work Analysis	Workforce Planning to Include Contingent Workers	From Talent Review to Talent Portfolio Review
HR Agility Process Audit™ -- Sample of HR Processes				
Anticipate Change	• Scan horizon for trends/forces of change • Actively monitor competitors • Maintain trend monitoring system – including early warning system • Regularly recalibrate focus based on trends • Build flexibility for rapid change • Introduce market defining paradigm shifts			
Generate Confidence	• Communicate clear vision & mission • Build teams & cross-functional collaboration • Create culture of employee engagement • Continually check priorities and resources for alignment • Actively communicate via multiple methods • Give and seek feedback about change • Ensure integrity & honesty			
Initiate Action	• Align priorities, resources & accountabilities • Make fast decisions based on emerging trends • Seek solutions from all levels – even front line • Shorten cycle times in all processes • Make speed of learning a competitive advantage • Demonstrate resilient capability in all areas • Apply plug and play action teams			
Liberate Thinking	• Create empowering environment that fosters fresh, innovative thinking at all times • Continuously search new ways to communicate and collaborate with customers • Make creative and effective use of ideas expressed by others – encourage involvement throughout • Continually seek use of new technology, processes and alliances			
Evaluate Results	• Scorecards continually reviewed for data concerning key processes • Systems provide rapid feedback on changing conditions • Coaching provided for on-going improvement • After action reviews quickly inform key decisions • Key metrics are aligned with rewards			

Illustration of Work Analysis -- Process mapping is used to identify the tasks and flow of work which should be accomplished by full-time employees and which ones could be done by contingent workers.

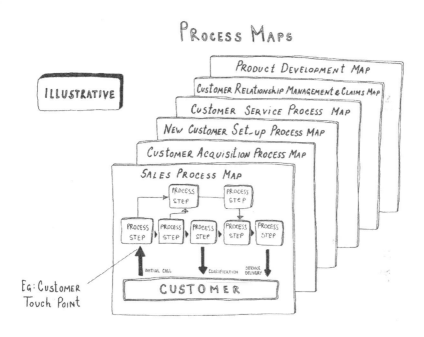

PROCESS MAPS

ILLUSTRATIVE

PRODUCT DEVELOPMENT MAP

CUSTOMER RELATIONSHIP MANAGEMENT & CLAIMS MAP

CUSTOMER SERVICE PROCESS MAP

NEW CUSTOMER SET-UP PROCESS MAP

CUSTOMER ACQUISITION PROCESS MAP

SALES PROCESS MAP

Eg: CUSTOMER Touch Point

CUSTOMER

The matrix illustrated here, represents the types of questions used to identify the degree to which the Talent Planning process represents the entire Talent Portfolio or is solely focused on internal employee talent. It establishes a baseline of the changes needed to implement a comprehensive Talent Portfolio Planning process.

Nicholas F. Horney, Ph.D.　　111

HR Agility Process Audit™ -- Planning for The Gig Economy (Illustration)		
Agility Drivers	Key Agility Processes	Talent Portfolio Planning (0-100 Points)
Anticipate Change	• Scan horizon for trends/forces of change • Actively monitor competitors • Maintain trend monitoring system • Regularly recalibrate focus based on trends • Build flexibility for rapid change • Introduce market defining paradigm shifts	• Are we ready to discuss shifting from job analysis to work analysis? • How rigorous is HR in identifying areas where on-demand talent are required? • What critical capabilities are best achieved through on-demand talent? • How well has HR defined the scope of initiatives for on-demand talent? • How is the mix of the talent portfolio determined? • How does Human Resources continuously update the organization's shifting talent portfolio based on trends and patterns impacting the organization's strategy?
Generate Confidence	• Communicate clear vision & mission • Build teams & cross-functional collaboration • Create culture of employee engagement • Continually check priorities for alignment • Actively communicate via multiple methods • Give and seek feedback about change • Ensure integrity & honesty	• How has HR been involved in defining performance expectations for the talent portfolio? • How well is performance measured and discussed across your entire talent portfolio? • How has HR equipped management to effectively manage their talent portfolio? • What is the organization's strategy on talent deployment for maximum business impact? • How are capability gaps of the talent portfolio resources identified? • How confident is the organization that its talent portfolio management process is dynamic and reflects the fluid nature of our business environment?
Initiate Action	• Align priorities, resources & accountabilities • Make fast decisions based on emerging trends • Shorten cycle times in all processes • Make speed of learning a competitive advantage • Demonstrate resilient capability in all areas • Apply plug and play action teams	• How does HR proactively address the management of its talent portfolio? • How has HR proactively addressed conflicts between internal and external talent? • How fast can the organization flex its talent portfolio to meet VUCA demands? • How does the organization use recruitment and selection information to form early development plans for its talent portfolio? • How do individuals receive feedback from others beyond their direct manager? • How does the organization strengthen relationships in its talent environment?
Liberate Thinking	• Create empowering environment that fosters fresh, innovative thinking • Continuously search new ways to communicate and collaborate • Make creative and effective use of ideas expressed by others • Continually seek use of new technology, processes and alliances	• How is HR creatively addressing the cultural fit of its talent portfolio? • What does the onboarding process look like for the talent portfolio? • How does the HR department build skills in talent portfolio management to be able to offer targeted assistance to the organization? • What does the organization do to provide the individual with a formal opportunity to share his or her perspectives on the organization?
Evaluate Results	• Scorecards continually reviewed for data concerning key processes • Systems provide rapid feedback on changing conditions • Coaching provided for on-going improvement • After action reviews conducted • Key metrics are aligned with rewards	• How bureaucratic are the HR policies in dealing with external talent? How engaged are the external talent compared to full-time employees? • How are the long-term costs of not developing the talent portfolio determined? • How does the succession management process include a review of how well leaders are deployed to realize strategic priorities? • How accountable is line management for the results of its talent portfolio? • How does the organization learn from talent portfolio management in order to support dissemination of best practices?
Totals		

©Agility Consulting

Step 2. Generate confidence in the changes necessary to thrive in a Hybrid Work Design – Equip managers with the training and coaching to better understand how to more effectively lead in a Gig Economy where functional and project teams include contingent workers, consultants and full-time employees. An important element of the management training would include the updated process for conducting the talent review for high potentials as noted in the graphic below.

VUCA Masters:
Developing Leadership Agility Fitness for the New World of Work

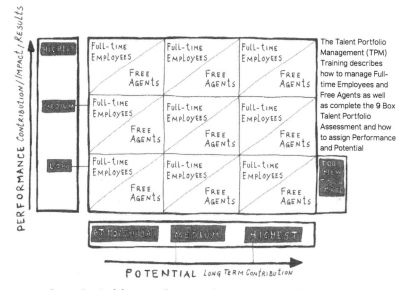

The Talent Portfolio Management (TPM) Training describes how to manage Full-time Employees and Free Agents as well as complete the 9 Box Talent Portfolio Assessment and how to assign Performance and Potential

Step 3. Initiate action to change the policies, processes, and philosophies of HR which relied on the assumption that organizational talent only consisted of internal full-time employees.

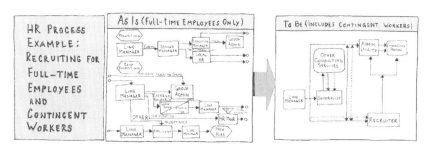

As described earlier, work analysis would include process mapping to identify the current and future tasks in each HR process. The illustration above provides the detailed tasks for the current recruiting process and the improved process focused on the entire talent portfolio. As this is a process that is continual and on-going, the ability to alter processes and structures quickly is vital. This element is fundamentally about process improvement in HR processes to better equip HR for the Gig Economy.

Nicholas F. Horney, Ph.D.   113

Step 4. Liberate thinking by creating the environment for the HR Team to think creatively about the how to redesign HR processes, policies and philosophies supportive of the Hybrid Work. The graphic below illustrate a Talent Review Process Example by applying scenario planning to the Talent Review process where contingent workers would also be reviewed for performance and potential so that the organization's entire talent portfolio can be identified and developed. Talent Portfolio mix of full-time and contingent workers. Combinations of talent are likely to vary depending upon the strategic planning business scenario.

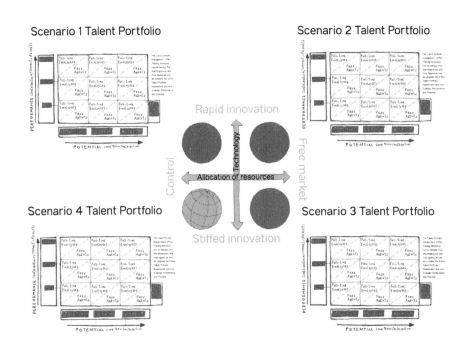

Step 5. Evaluate results – What impact has the transformation to support Hybrid Work impacted key performance indicators of Human Resources? Key performance indicators as represented in the graphic below are illustrations of results which can be tracked and monitored to determine if the CHRO's HR Agility initiatives are having the desired impact on the organization.

VUCA Masters:
Developing Leadership Agility Fitness for the New World of Work

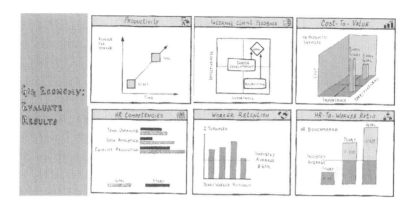

Interview with Mary Eckenrod, former Chief Learning Officer with Blackberry and Lenovo. What are some of the actions which CHROs need to be proactively taking to address the challenges of the New World of Work?

- Understand company workforce practices and policies impacting independent workers
- Understand regulatory restrictions impacting independent workers in countries where you employ talent
- Accelerate initiatives to identify and keep your best talent (project work, rotations, flexibility, and collaboration)
- Map and incorporate new demands for leaders into leadership development
- Broaden your workforce plan to include more external talent
- Build collaborative processes and plans with talent acquisition and procurement
- Think differently about a "career" in your organization
- Start with a functional sponsor to build process and expertise
- Educate your senior management on the New Workforce

Nicholas F. Horney, Ph.D.   115

Leadership and Team Agility in the New World of Work

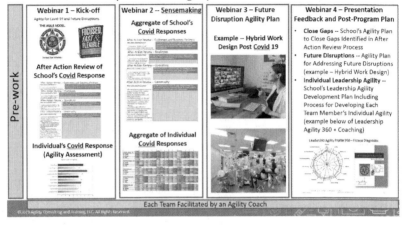

We have used an After Action Agility process similar to the graphic illustrated above to work with clients to conduct an After Action Review of how their organization applied agility before, during and after Covid-19. A combination of organizational actions and individual leadership actions were documented and analyzed. Client teams applied what was learned from the Covid-19 After Action Review process and applied their learning through the lens of The Agile Model® to future disruptions like the implementation of a hybrid work design for their business.

One client introduced a 3x5 card to help reinforce a mindset and culture of agility all meetings held (e.g., departmental, project, etc.). Each meeting planned would be structured around the 5 Drivers represented in The Agile Model® to reinforce a common language about agility. Very few leaders found it difficult to adjust their meeting agendas to align and reinforce a mindset of agility.

VUCA Masters:
Developing Leadership Agility Fitness for the New World of Work

Recommended Leadership Agility Fitness Actions for the New World of Work

Anticipating Change -- refers to your ability to interpret the potential impact of business turbulence and trends along with the implications to the enterprise.

Anticipating Change requires effective capabilities for Visioning, Sensing and Monitoring. Below, you'll find definitions for these capabilities along with suggestions for development and potential consequences of over-reliance.

Visioning -- refers to your capability to create a clear mental picture of what could be and how to succeed.

1. Volunteer to explain and field questions at an inter-functional meeting on how your department's goals support those of the organization. This will test your understanding of the topic and increase your knowledge.

2. Schedule a virtual retreat for your team in order to take the time away from the office to address strategic issues for the unit. Use the retreat to develop and get agreement about a practical plan of action. This kind of activity will signal to your employees the importance of the company's vision and values and encourage others to think about how they can apply a broader perspective into their daily activities.

3. Regularly visiting, in-person or virtually, company units and ensure you listen to the employees to get a feel for the operation. Take every opportunity you can to reinforce your vision for the future and try to help individuals understand how they can help to achieve it.

4. Identify factors that are blocking or impeding the implementation of company's vision, and work with others to develop an action plan to remove or get around these barriers. Set a schedule for each of these actions plans, publicize the details throughout the company and maintain accountability for results in a public forum.

5. Create a hypothetical crisis scenario for your organization. Document the steps that you think would be most appropriate for you to take. Think through as many consequences or outcomes as you can and rationalize why certain actions would likely be the best. This exercise will help you to think through more slowly an ideal action plan for a crisis situation and may help you determine alternatives when a real situation occurs.

Nicholas F. Horney, Ph.D.   117

6. Disseminate your hypothetical scenario with your team and ask them for their input around the best course of action. Ask what they would expect to see you do and how a person in your position should act. Compare and contrast your initial solutions with those of the group to better understand how perceptions can color outcomes in crisis situations.

7. Develop contingency plans that can be implemented if things do not go as planned. Develop plans to accommodate several potential courses of action. This will force you to think through alternative scenarios as well as solutions on a regular basis.

8. Take the initiative to participate in strategic business planning discussions and processes. Establish a leading role in writing and contributing to a strategic business plan for the company that utilizes more advanced business and industry concepts. Take on the task of conceptually integrating the plans of separate functional areas in the written plan. This kind of participation will expose you to more complex and conceptual problems and develop your ability to integrate data.

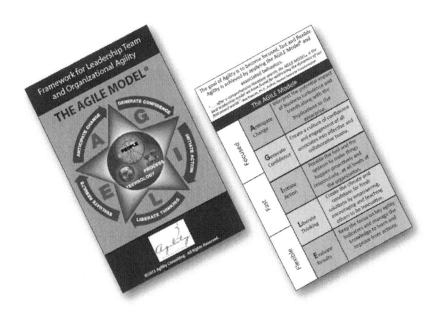

VUCA Masters:
Developing Leadership Agility Fitness for the New World of Work

Sensing -- refers to your capability to draw upon diverse sources of information to recognize the subtle signs of impending change.

9. Looking at the future business strategy, examine the broader future development needs of your team. Working with the team, identify the main areas required for development across the group and then put appropriate development plans into action.

10. Examine where the company is going in the next year and determine what obstacles under your control may impede this progress. Clearly identify and enact a quarterly plan to avoid such pitfalls.

11. From the quarterly plan evaluate whether you will have the skills to meet these needs and then identify areas where you need development. Implement a systematic plan to achieve your development goals.

12. Create a knowledge management system by maintaining information on emerging ideas and changes in the business. Make a list of the opportunities that will result from these changes. Map out, in detail, the steps you need to take in order to capitalize on these opportunities and after thorough analysis make key business decisions.

13. Review recent situations where you have not adapted well or where you found change difficult. Identify what made this so difficult, and work out ways of dealing with these types of situations in the future. This will challenge you to adapt quickly.

14. Convene virtual forums using Zoom Meetings in which employees can challenge the plans, provide new ideas or ask clarifying questions. Circulate ideas for change in advance of implementation. Communicate openly and honestly in order to anticipate and understand the impact that these changes are likely to have.

15. Develop a list of the skills in your department with notes about level of ability and readiness to take on new tasks and delegate tasks which explicitly link to an individual's development plan and the skills of the person. Then conduct follow-up with employees to make sure that tasks are being completed correctly.

16. Develop a plan for identifying possible areas of change, along with a plan for exploiting "crisis" situations that were not anticipated. This can be done by identifying areas of strength and being able to utilize those elements for unanticipated chaotic situations.

Monitoring -- refers to your capability to systematically identify and organize data regarding key trends that impact the organization.

17. Identify your top five competitors and conduct research to learn more about their operations. Think about what differentiates your company and how your performance could support that. Share your findings with others to obtain feedback and assist others to improve.

18. Gather benchmark information. Make a systematic attempt to find out how others within and outside of your organization have dealt with similar situations or problems. Making this effort over time will encourage you to look for innovative solutions and to understand how the same problem can produce different impacts.

19. Review the status of each of your key projects. Identify current problems, missing or incomplete information and potential obstacles that may arise. For each of these areas, outline and begin to implement an action plan to address the issue. This will help you get used to recognizing problem areas and develop a more integrated picture of how various issues impact your projects.

20. Develop a strategy for reducing risks. For example, some risks can be reduced by good planning. Identify the "go/no go" decision points so that you know when the risk becomes too great. Using this technique will help you make risky decisions more quickly and increase your comfort with making risky decisions.

21. Subscribe to journals in your field and industry that discuss new developments. Use your reading to generate ideas about potential new, cutting-edge projects. Explore these possibilities with others in order to initiate a positive impact on the work unit.

22. Keep a record of problems that arise. Analyze these problems to identify interrelated themes and to look for root causes. By keeping records, you will be able to identify similarities between situations more quickly and efficiently, and have a greater ability to identify longer-term solutions to recurring problems.

23. Streamline any data collection systems, to include communication modes. This will allow for more efficient use of resources by eliminating duplicate efforts and errors in collection or transmission.

24. Develop systematic processes that align performance measure data being collected to that of strategic objectives and quantifiable action plans.

Generating Confidence -- refers to your ability to create a culture of confidence and engagement with all stakeholders, especially associates in effective and collaborative teams.

Generating Confidence requires effective capabilities for Connecting, Aligning and Engaging. Below, you'll find definitions for these capabilities along with suggestions for development and potential consequences of over-reliance.

Connecting -- refers to your capability to clearly link people's work with strategic objectives in a way that inspires progress.

1. Clearly articulate strategic business objectives throughout the organization. Ensure that interdepartmental goals visibly align for a holistic approach within the organization. By including all departments, one can eliminate redundancies.

2. After discussing it with your manager, take the initiative in preparing and presenting a case study of a work situation to your colleagues at a staff meeting. Discuss what happened and what might have been a more appropriate resolution of the situation given the goals of the organization.

3. Solicit input on team goals from your employees. Ask your employees for suggestions and ideas about how the team can best meet its goals and contribute to departmental or organizational goals. This will reinforce to everyone what those goals are and develop practical ac-

tivities to achieve personal objectives aligned with those goals.

4. Celebrate team accomplishments that align with strategic objectives. Plan activities and festivities to celebrate the accomplishment of team goals. Reward every member of the team when this occurs. Include activities that develop or build upon a team identity or team tradition. This will enhance team morale and cohesion.

5. Set one goal for yourself each week that will contribute to your annual objectives. Take time at the end of each week to review how you contributed to attaining that goal. By continually reminding yourself of your long-term goals while setting shorter-term targets you will develop the ability to stay focused and productive.

6. Utilize a current performance measurement system to plan and track elements towards business objectives. This will allow objective measures of successful completion of tasks and can aid in then develop of new ones.

7. Coaching can serve as a way to provide feedback on performance objectives towards goal attainment in between evaluation cycles for employees. This can also serve to build up supervisory experience among managers.

8. Increase performance accountability through assignment of greater responsibility and assigning mentorship. This will allow for individuals to attain more skills, along with having feedback provided concerning their contribution to the organization.

Aligning refers to your capability to adapt what gets done and how people do it to maintain congruence with reality.

9. Practice identifying similarities between your opinion and that of others before pointing out differences of opinion. Point out these similarities to display that you are listening intently and understand the other individual's perspective.

10. Listen to get a clear understanding of another person's perceptions of a situation. Then express to the individual your sense of what they are thinking and feeling. Listening and showing empathy will contribute significantly to success, not only in negotiations and people

management, but also where frequent contact with people from other countries and cultures calls for recognition of their values and concerns.

11. Identify your own natural leadership and management style and the styles needed by your staff. Identify the unique issues, concerns and motivators of each of your employees. Make a conscious effort to adapt your own behavior to best respond to those motivators and needs.

12. Ask team members for advice in areas where they have expertise or experience and, when appropriate, to share their expertise at team meetings. This will expand your knowledge and help identify areas of strength and weakness on the team.

13. Identify and remove obstacles to effective performance. Identify factors that are blocking or impeding your performance and develop a plan to remove or get around these barriers. Implement the plan. Systematically identifying problems you will be able to identify similarities between various situations and derive solutions more rapidly.

14. Be cognizant of times when you immediately shoot down ideas and consider what mental schema is influencing your reaction to certain ideas. Challenging these will improve your awareness and leadership abilities.

15. If you find yourself constantly referring to manuals, policies, and regulations as opposed to critical thinking or impromptu decision making in situations, consider why. Would you better be able to progress and develop yourself and organization if you allowed more flexibility in planning and decision making?

16. Are you continuously seeking out resources for learning and development, along with presenting the opportunities for growth for managers and employees?

Engaging refers to your capability to build an emotional connection with the organization that sparks productivity and commitment.

17. When others are speaking, notice any tendencies you have to drift off or to do anything other than listen. To focus on listening, use appropriate skills such as paraphrasing, asking relevant questions and using non-verbal

signals. This will develop your listening skills by forcing you to concentrate on what others have to say.

18. After conversations or interactions with others, attempt to make a prioritized list of what is important to them. Check this list with the individual to assess your performance. This type of practice will help you develop your listening skills.

19. Ask others open-ended questions that require more than simple "yes" and "no" responses. Use the answers to probe for individual's interests and goals. By listening and evaluating people in this fashion you will enhance your understanding of others and your listening skills.

20. Focus on both verbal and non-verbal clues conveyed by your audience. Listen to what people say but also focus on how they act. Do they lose eye contact? What about their facial expressions? By utilizing this information you will be able to gain a greater understanding of their opinions.

21. Develop your ability to make small talk. Greet people warmly and take the time to discuss personal concerns with them. Create an environment that encourages openness and trust so that when confronted with a stressful situation, the person feels that he/she can ask for help.

22. Say thank you regularly. Try to thank your peers, subordinates, support staff and any external agencies for help that they give you on a consistent basis. This can be done speaking face-to-face, using the telephone, writing a note or memo or in any other creative manner. The gesture will be appreciated because it will help to communicate your respect for others' work.

23. Regularly recognize each team member by delivering positive feedback to each person at least once per week. Use a variety of different methods to deliver the feedback (e.g., phone, in person, thank you note, at team meeting) and to set a positive example for others.

24. Let team members plan and conduct portions of meetings. Give them complete responsibility for selected portions of the agenda, provide assistance as necessary and give them feedback after the meeting to help develop leadership skills in others.

25. At meetings, encourage team members to comment on issues or offer ideas by recording comments on a virtual white board. Contribute your own views, but in general, say as little as possible. This will help you learn about others' expertise and build overall team involvement.

26. Help employees think through approaches. Ask an employee to present the advantages and disadvantages of several alternative approaches to a critical situation, and recommend a specific plan of action before you voice your own opinion. Coach employees by asking questions such as "What if you did it this way?" rather than directing their actions.

Initiating Action refers to your ability to provide the fuel and the systems to enable things to happen proactively and responsively, at all levels of the organization.

Initiating Action requires effective capabilities for Bias for Action, Decision Making and Collaborating. Below, you'll find definitions for these capabilities along with suggestions for development and potential consequences of over-reliance.

Bias for Action refers to your capability to take charge with a sense of urgency in proactively evaluating and responding to situations.

1. Establish an individual time within which you will make decisions and stick to it. By setting and adhering to specific time frames you will be developing your ability to act in a timely and decisive fashion.

2. After listening to others or gathering information, communicate how you feel about an issue or interaction simply and clearly, without being indirect or backing off. Assertiveness is an important component of being decisive. It is important that you practice taking a direct approach when expressing yourself.

3. Make a list of all the decisions that you have put off over the last few months. Set yourself a schedule to make decisions on all the issues and keep to it. It is important that you don't let problems or issues linger. By establishing this schedule you will be more likely to act on unresolved issues.

4. Use flow diagrams to trace potential origins of problems, and alternate solutions. Evaluate the cost/benefit of the alternatives, taking time into account and commit to a course of action within a given time frame. This diagram should help you visualize problems, solutions and alternatives and as a result, assist you in the decision making process.

5. Identify a customer issue on which immediate action is necessary or the opportunity will be lost. Utilize your network of resources to gather some important information. However, where information is incomplete focus on the essential variable and utilize what you know about them to make a rapid rationale decision. In the face of incomplete information it is important that you practice focusing on the most essential pieces of information when making a decision.

6. Work with a person who demonstrates a high level of initiative. Discuss how he/she identifies events in which initiative can be taken. Others' input can broaden your options by identifying ideas you had not previously considered.

7. Identify current business opportunities that can be seized immediately. Develop a systematic plan of action which includes a timetable for taking advantage of these possibilities, and then enact this plan.

8. Seek feedback from others on how you convey a sense of urgency for projects and tasks. Solicit specific information about when you have displayed appropriate urgency, when you have shown inappropriate urgency and any patterns they have observed. Conveying a sense of importance that's consistent with the priority of the task/project increases the likelihood that others will take immediate action when needed.

9. Develop an action plan for your team to improve internal and external processes. Review this with your team, asking for input. Be as concrete as possible about how the change translates into daily work, and periodically review the progress of the team in adapting to the changes.

Decision Making refers to your capability to create solutions at the right time, with the right frameworks and at the right organizational level.

10. Share decision-making. Ask your subordinates to participate in making major decisions with you. Give them whatever information you have about the issues facing the organization and then encourage them to decide how, collectively, you can best respond to those issues.

11. Look for problem solving situations. Identify problems that affect you but that are not your responsibility and assert yourself by making contributions and coming up with solutions. This will increase your analytic and problem-solving capabilities which will, in turn, increase your willingness to take on even more complex assignments.

12. Provide a clear rationale for your decisions and actions. Explain the "whys" to subordinates in a way that clearly links decisions and actions to your strategic vision, priorities and objectives in order to gain commitment and provide clear leadership.

13. Use a system to detail ideas and information, such as: ordering chronologically, in order of importance, in terms of positive benefits and negative benefits, or in terms of meeting a long-term goal. By developing a system, you will be able to review all of the information more thoroughly and with more clarity before making decisions.

14. Make sincere attempts to avoid drawing conclusions too quickly based on the immediately available information or internalized concepts you bring into specific situations. Make sure that you take enough time to gather sufficient detailed information to develop a factual basis for your decisions.

15. Identify the most crucial decisions with long-term impact that you have to make this quarter. Map out the ideal process for making those decisions and any obstacles to pursuing those processes. Share your proposals with others you respect to get their input, and stay as close to the ideal processes as possible when making the decision.

16. Analyze past decisions to determine how collecting less information or taking less time would have changed the decision. Identify what would have changed the decision. Identify what you could have done differently to speed up the decision process. Analyzing past decisions is an excellent way to help you identify your decision-making strengths and weaknesses. You can then use this information for personal development.

17. Use tools and information that you have on potential profit, return on assets or competitive pricing when analyzing options. After you have identified your alternatives in the face of uncertainty, make it a habit to think through the criteria upon which you should select the appropriate course of action.

18. Learn and use analytical techniques such as force field analysis, "mind-mapping," fishbone analysis, SWOT analysis. Increase your use of statistical techniques and computer tools that allow you to see relationships between different factors. This will help you more quickly absorb, manage and understand large amounts of data.

Collaborating refers to your capability to actively create partners and find common ground across groups to achieve common goals.

19. Make a master list of people who can provide assistance or information. By preparing a list of resources you will be raising your awareness of the individuals who are capable of helping you avoid the pitfalls.

20. Work on cross-functional projects. Get involved in projects that involve people from other areas of the organization. Through this interaction you should gain a broader perspective of goals and activities outside your function.

21. Hold information-sharing virtual meetings. Keep others involved and well informed about organizational issues affecting them by holding frequent meetings to share information and ideas. By providing information and exploring others' ideas about how to improve team and/or department results, you can begin to build a more effective team.

22. Identify two members of your team who need to work well together to meet a particular project's objectives, but who appear, for whatever reason, to be in conflict. Meet with each person informally and ask each individual what is at the root of the problem. In particular, find out what each party would like the other to do differently to enable the team as a whole to achieve its objectives.

23. When working with people in other business functions, even when engaged in task-related discussions, place extra emphasis on listening actively. Demonstrate this attentiveness by seeking points of agreement and make an effort to point out the similarities, not just differences. Indicating areas of consensus will demonstrate that you were listening and share similar ideas.

24. Utilize the organizations strategy for outlining goals towards engaging in partnerships. This should include defined roles for all parties, program resources, and requirements for successful collaboration.

25. Foster a culture that exudes coordination and inclusion, for expressing collaborative efforts and enhancing acceptance of internal and external forms of partnership. Effective partner engagement requires a culture of coordination and inclusion.

26. Ensure access to appropriate leadership at all times, displaying transparency in all engagements. Seek to comply with other organizations business operating styles, while incorporating their strengths into plans.

27. Engage in project and team management training in order to attain knowledge and skills required to foster collaborative efforts.

28. Partners in efforts relate to one another in a non-hierarchical basis, with no one person "in charge". Ensure no single unit within any given organization controls or dominates decision making or resource appropriation.

Liberating Thinking refers to your ability to create the climate and conditions for fresh innovative solutions by empowering, encouraging, teaching and expecting others to be innovative.

Liberating Thinking requires effective capabilities for Bias for Innovation, Customer Focus and Idea Diversity. Below, you'll find definitions for these capabilities along with suggestions for development and potential consequences of over-reliance.

Bias for Innovation refers to your capability to support novel, useful solutions and unconventional approaches that challenge the status quo.

1.   Ask an individual that has just entered your organization to identify the differences he/she sees between your organization and their past employer. This will give you a new (outside) opinion on what is unique about your organizational culture. An "outside" or new perspective often helps you identify issues previously overlooked.

2.   Make team problem solving part of every team meeting. Identify an important problem or opportunity from the team, and ask each employee to come to the unit meeting with 2-3 ideas for dealing with the issue. This will encourage others to suggest ideas and contribute to the process.

3.   Create a team in your functional area and have team members brainstorm opportunities for enhancing the function's performance. Encourage the group to develop and implement an action plan to seize these opportunities.

4.   Write a list of some of the work processes or systems that you are dissatisfied with. Then spend time talking to various people and gaining different perspectives around the issues. Try to be as creative as possible in looking for ways to improve these systems.

5.   Champion the creation of a new idea or process. Hold an internal contest to find the most creative solution to an ongoing problem. Provide the resources and support to develop the winning idea, reward the participants and provide an opportunity for the plan to be presented to the whole team to act as an example.

6. Take any innovative idea that has been recently implemented unsuccessfully by your team, and identify what were the key factors that caused the lack of success. Now work with your team to identify the key learnings from this experience and to understand how they could be applied to push the organization forward in the future.

7. Engage in industry foresight, where forces driving change have been identified, trends are tracked, new technologies are utilized, and alternative scenarios are considered.

8. Encourage a work environment that allocates innovation time, but also emphasizes volume, iteration planning, and speed. This will allow for more ideas to be elicited, yet eliminate the time and cost waste for ones that do not come to fruition.

9. Allow for creative failure. Create an organization that recognizes failure in regards to innovation as successful attempts at a better product or service.

Customer Focus refers to your capability to seek greater understanding of customers' needs and use that knowledge to fuel solutions.

10. Gather information on the history of a key customer's organization to begin to improve your understanding of various underlying or political forces/influences.

11. Conduct a regular survey of customers to determine their level of satisfaction. By gathering information in a proactive fashion you can prevent many mistakes and enhance customer satisfaction.

12. Act quickly when the customer expresses dissatisfaction. Follow up with a personal call to discuss the problem and let the customer know what is being done to correct or improve the situation. Responsiveness and personal attention make the customer feel valued by your organization.

13. Set yourself a series of guidelines for handling customer requests (e.g., return customer calls and e-mails within 24 hours, ask at the end of a request if you can do anything else, etc.), and then strive to meet them in every customer interaction.

14. Visit your team's customers in other departments and seek to understand their requirements and how they will use your input. Utilize this information when providing service. This will enable you to gather important information, and it will convey to your customer that you are interested in what they have to say.

15. Examine your customers' industry. Identify the competitive pressures they face. Use this information to tailor your service so that you are more successful at meeting their needs.

16. Identify a list of your customers' strategic business needs, and prepare a plan for meeting them. Convey this information to your co-workers and superiors so that your entire organization can begin acting with greater customer orientation. By educating yourself and then your organization you will be advocating an entirely new corporate approach toward customer service.

17. Work with customers as a partner in their business planning process. This type of partnering demonstrates that you are more valuable than simply the products you provide, and as a result, the customer will be more eager to foster your relationship.

18. Meet with your customers virtually and in informal settings. Begin to explore on a nondirective basis those ideas that will help you better accomplish their goals. By your demonstrating a sincere interest in their affairs, customers are likely to be more interested and loyal to you and your organization.

Idea Diversity refers to your capability to seek many perspectives when solving problems and create a safe climate for sharing thoughts.

19. Create a case study for yourself by identifying a region or country in which your company has enjoyed limited success. Learn as much as you can about the circumstances, and analyze how you would deal with the situation. This will help expose you to situations in which the competition and environment are different from what you are used to.

20. Invite others in the organization, such as senior management or employees external to your department, to speak at your virtual staff meetings about what other areas are doing to improve performance and better align their activities with the objectives of the company as a whole.

21. Know what's happening in your organization. Read company literature, and take advantage of informal opportunities to communicate with people throughout the organization. This sort of interaction allows you to get others' perspectives on how things get done within the organization.

22. Float ideas. Ask others to listen to an idea you have developed or that has occurred to you and press them to consider the merits. By continually presenting new ideas you will become more comfortable trying innovative approaches.

23. Suggest brainstorming sessions with your team or others whenever possible in order to hear and help generate numerous ideas or solutions. Do not evaluate or critique any of the ideas until you have exhausted all ideas. The purpose of this exercise is to stimulate creative ideas and break out of traditional ways of thinking.

24. Encourage creative brainstorming by setting up quality improvement teams. Reward the group for generating ideas that lead to even small quality improvements. This will reinforce and stimulate the group to generate other ideas that may lead to more substantial benefits.

25. Invite people external to either your unit or organization who have a reputation for being creative or innovative to virtual team meetings. Facilitate this as an interactive session, and try to draw out the common patterns or threads that led to the creation of new ideas. Emphasize to the group that not all new ideas work and that experimentation is acceptable.

26. Communicate your support for creativity consistently to your employees. Ask them to describe the actions that they have taken to foster creativity in others. Include this as a measure when evaluating their performance and assigning rewards.

27. When dealing with a changing situation where the solution you would typically use no longer works, brainstorm with a group of people to develop as many alternatives as you can. This will help you recognize how a change in a process or approach can lead to beneficial results.

28. Whenever you are involved in a project, map the solution out visually and systematically trace the implications it may have on other people or departments. Share your concerns with individuals in those areas and ask for their feedback. By doing this you will help yourself think outside your current paradigm.

Evaluating Results refers to your ability to maintain a strong focus and feedback system to continuously learn and improve from actions and changing dynamics.

Evaluating Results requires effective capabilities for Creating Expectations, Real-Time Feedback and Fact-Based Measures. Below, you'll find definitions for these capabilities along with suggestions for development and potential consequences of over-reliance.

Creating Expectations refers to your capability to clarify outcomes to guide performance and quality standards for people and teams.

1. Become a mentor to one or more individuals in your office. Discuss issues of ethics and professional values with them regularly and take a role in influencing their development and fostering ethical behavior.

2. When mistakes are made, focus on the solution and do not place blame. Conversely, hold yourself to a higher standard. When you make a mistake or might be responsible for a misunderstanding, acknowledge it and make a public apology. This will help to foster an atmosphere of trust and provide others with a behavioral role model.

3. Ask for team members' input when developing agendas for meetings to ensure that all important issues can be addressed. Distribute copies of the meeting agenda and any other pertinent information in advance, and quickly review the agenda again with the group at the start of the meetings. This exercise will help to improve overall clarity for the team and keep everyone involved in developing the group process.

4. Place greater emphasis on setting key functional priorities, enlisting others when necessary to achieve major goals and expecting results from your immediate team members or other employees. This will set the bar for a results orientation within the team and ensure that things get done.

5. Focus on identifying practical details and situational demands when setting work priorities. Work against the tendency to establish and follow up pre-conceived goals, plans and strategies that do not take into account the more mundane, daily details that must be addressed for a successful outcome. This exercise will help you to make realistic and rational decisions while maintaining exposure to alternatives.

6. Write SMART objectives (Specific, Measurable, Attainable, Results-Oriented, Timely). Identify and discuss the end results of key job requirements ("to have increased/developed") and success indicators (time, quantity, quality, behavior). Discuss how and why these are important.

7. Ensure clarity about performance goals and expectations by meeting with employees to set goals. Ask your employees to summarize, in writing, your agreements about performance expectations and to give you a copy. Discuss anything you disagree with or think needs to be added in order to increase clarity.

8. Develop a model or system by which to judge all employees' work. Use this model to increase consistency in work assessments and to enable employees to self-assess themselves and improve their own performance.

9. Practice alignment for employees in regards to performance expectations and systems of recognition. This will serve as a link for employees to understand missions and accomplishment of individual efforts.

10. Articulate accountability, either through meetings, evaluations, or other communication means. This will engage employees and elicit commitment to specific tasks if they know they will be checked on the outcome.

Real Time Feedback refers to your capability to guide improvement by supporting an open environment for sharing observations about behavior.

11. Create a forum within which ideas are solicited from employees regarding how company can best realize its objectives and priorities. Facilitate meetings in which employees can express their ideas, thoughts, feelings and concerns.

12. Set up regular meetings where others have an opportunity to express their concerns about work practices or processes. Practice your questioning and probing techniques to gain a full understanding of their perspectives.

13. Seek feedback from others on your ability to meet commitments. Ask them for specific examples of incidents in which you were both successful and unsuccessful in meeting a commitment. This will help you to recognize the behaviors and situations that lead to certain outcomes so that you can work at adapting your style.

14. Provide data/information to your team that will help them with their roles. Consider information about products, customers, markets, regulations or the industry. Analyze data available internally and communicate your findings, or disseminate information from external sources.

15. Provide clear, timely feedback to employees. Let them know what they are doing well and what they are not doing to meet your expectations. In either case, be specific about what behavior should or should not continue, and why. By doing this on a regular, ongoing basis, employees will begin to recognize your standards and expectations more quickly and accurately.

16. At quarterly reviews, ask whether the practical needs of the team are being met. Solicit feedback about what you can do to enhance team productivity and job satisfaction. Based on this feedback, pursue needed information, personnel or other resources that will help the team meet its objectives.

17. Become aware. If individuals within your organization are silent, they are likely holding something back. Be cognizant of non-verbal cues such as these and immediately address the root cause.

18. Options. Individuals who are provided options feel will more likely engage in a feedback loop. Some people are more timid and will not speak up in a group setting, therefore, you must adjust and have one on one meetings, or elicit more casual conversations.

19. Create a culture of ownership. Include managers and other employees in high level meetings that include financial and strategic planning, so they can have a feeling of inclusion in the success or failure of the organization.

Fact Based Measures refers to your capability to use data as evidence to understand issues, evaluate options, form conclusions and make decisions.

20. Conduct a review of the department's expenditures against budget to date. Determine the expenditure that enhanced the cost-effectiveness of the department and expenditure that gave no tangible benefit. This activity will help you better use business principles and tools at the departmental level.

21. Analyze the cost structure of a project you are managing and what it is costing the organization. By identifying the cost drivers you will be more able to control or influence these factors and thereby increase profits.

22. When possible, quantify organizational goals. Design graphical representations of these goals, your department's ongoing results in these areas and any competitor information you can find. Update, display and review these results with your unit regularly and ask for specific suggestions around continually improving performance.

23. Assess the costs and benefits of a plan, and of each of the steps within the plan. Consider both tangible and intangible costs and benefits. Analyze optimistic, conservative and pessimistic versions of the plan. Support each version with appropriate back-up data.

24. Identify how the organization measures efficiency, productivity and quality in ways that are relevant to your area. Review your current projects or accountabilities and set goals based on achieving greater efficiency, productivity and quality. By setting goals you are mapping out a systematic plan to achieve your desired results.

25. When preparing an argument examine which types of hard evidence, such as facts and figures, can support your assertions. Search out that information and include it in your presentation. Data that support your argument are always valuable when attempting to influence others.

26. Establish specific month-to-month control measures for the projects you are managing. Inform others of your specific expectations including what is to be accomplished and by when.

27. Create decision systems as opposed to data systems, to where the process in itself supports the use of measurement. This will eliminate the collection of measurements that serve little to no purpose for the overall vision for the organization.

28. Assign duties to individual personnel or departments for establishing priorities and measurements that align with organizational goals. This creates an interconnectedness within the organization for data driven decision making.

Dave Cuthbert – VUCA Master

From suit to stubble beard - how a corporate CEO became a global change-maker

After ringing the bell on Wall Street when his company became a publicly traded company, David thought this was the highlight of his career. He never thought he would be building water wells in remote communities a couple of years later. But David's life changed drastically. This is his story - one about breaking with expectations and diving into the dark waters.

It was 2014, and in a 5-minute meeting, David got fired as the CEO of a big cloud technology company in Philadelphia. Up until then he had been an athlete, special operations officer, and a corporate executive. The Monday after he was fired, he went from receiving about 130 emails a day, to two emails - one from his mother and one from his aunt. They told them they were praying for him. "My aunt is a non, so that one definitely counted", David laughs.

His life paused. David was forced to listen to his intuition. He learned, took a few risks, spent some nights in a mosquito-infused cabin in Haiti, and found himself on a path more rewarding than he ever thought possible. "Like many who find themselves at a crossroads, I took stock of my life to determine what I really wanted it to be about."

"I thought I had everything figured out. But when the board of the company told me I was no longer their CEO, it felt like I stepped off the bullet train, while the train kept going. I stopped worrying about my inbox, because it was no longer there. I stopped worrying about my title, because it was no longer there. I stopped worrying about shareholders' expectations, because, within a day, none of them were there anymore. After I broke with those expectations and started to think about what I could do, rather than what I had to do, suddenly everything was possible. A couple of months later, I met a six-year-old boy in Haiti, and this meeting changed my life forever. There's a real opportunity in my story for companies. And I want to share that story."

"At the time, little did I know what this experience would become or how it would lead me to where I am today."

"It all started in high school. My guidance counselor came to me and suggested I apply for one of the military academies. I was shocked by the suggestion, since I had never considered it before. After some thought, I decided that if I was going to apply to a military academy, Navy would be the only option. My dad was in the Navy, my grandfather was in the Navy, even my great-great grandfather was. At the time, little did I know what this experience would become or how it would lead me to where I am today."

"We were preparing for battle with every single soccer game."

Hooked

A passion for teams and sports, some of his most transformative moments took place on the green grass of a soccer field. This has been a core part of his story from early in his life. "When I watch soccer, goals are great, but I focus on the buildup to a goal, the teamwork it takes to create that goal. It's beautiful. When I started playing soccer at the Naval Academy, I sat on the bench watching the others play, not part of the team I was dying to be a member of. It sucked. I knew I really only had one choice. And that was to improve my game. I fully committed myself to the improvement process and noticed that my efforts paid off quickly. Interestingly, what I also noticed was that my hard work and improvement made the team better. That's when I was hooked on the idea that my individual effort could help improve something beyond myself, even an entire team, and so can anyone else's.

"This was an important leadership lesson for me, even as a freshman. Because in the Academy, although we were playing soccer, we were also future Naval Officers. We were preparing for battle with every single soccer game. We had to get out and work toward a goal, performing at our best. Because in a combat environment, there's no other option than performing at your best-the stakes are too high. Therefore, you either work to improve, or you don't. I am fortunate that this is a lesson I learned at a relatively young age, and it has served me well ever since."

For David, the biggest motivator in the Navy was leading a team to greater heights than individuals can achieve on their own. It was like that when he was the captain of a soccer team at the Academy, and it was that way when he was sent on his first mission in Iraq. Successfully completing a complicated mission with a team, that was what it was all about.

"As I sat with my dive gear on the edge of the boat preparing to dive into blackness, I knew there could be no hesitation."

"Our very first mission was to disarm underwater mines in an Iraqi port, at nighttime. It felt like diving in a closed closet, just pitch black. As the leader of our team, although it was an uncertain and scary time, I knew I had to demonstrate confidence. I had to dive in first. I remember thinking as I sat with my dive gear on the edge of the boat preparing to dive into blackness, 'There can be no hesitation.' I had to trust my preparation and enter the water. This was another extremely valuable leadership lesson for me. I had to set the example and assure the team we were ready to take on the challenge. Leadership is uncomfortable at times, but maybe that's the point."

"The feeling went beyond losing my job or title. It felt like I lost my identity."

Two realities

After his time in the Navy, David became the CEO of a new tech company, and later the CEO of a publicly traded company from New York when the startup merged with an established telephone company. "Again, our team had a mission and a vision for the future. To stay competitive in the digital landscape, we had to rebrand our acquired company and scale up by merging with other technology companies. It quickly became clear our board did not support this vision. Caught between these two realities, I was in an extremely challenging leadership situation, probably the hardest of my professional career. I was in a position to lead the company to grow while knowing we did not have shared vision at the top. I felt totally committed to the team and to finding a way to continue success. Even so, in 2014, the board called me in and told me I was no longer their guy, we did not have the same expectations for the company. At the time, I did not see this as the serendipitous event that the passing of time has revealed it to be; it just felt like I had been punched in the stomach. The feeling went beyond losing my job or title. It felt like I lost my identity."

David took a month off to collect his thoughts and evaluate his path. And, on a Monday afternoon during that time, he and his wife spent the day at a vineyard contemplating what they would do next. As they were drinking wine, David watched a man in the vineyard pruning a grapevine.

"And that's when it hit me: he's stripping this vine from all its distractions, so it can produce the best wine possible."

"He was so meticulous about this single grapevine. As I was watching him, ten minutes passed, twenty minutes, half an hour... And that's when it hit me: he's stripping this vine from all its distractions, so it can produce the best wine possible. At that very moment, I was challenged to think about my own life in the same way. If all the noise, false identities, distractions, and status were removed, what would my life look like? What would the best version of myself look like?

"A couple of days later, I'm scrolling on my phone, and I see the Wine To Water CEO job description. Wine To Water was a small nonprofit in Boone, North Carolina, providing clean water solutions all over the world. The job asked for field experience, which I had over ten years of in the Navy. It also asked for organizational growth experience. I had just done that for nine years at the tech company. It seemed like this job was made for me, although it was a path I never saw coming."

"Billions of people lack access to clean water. But I could solve this problem for this kid, right now."

Moving the needle

"I drove down to North Carolina to see what this organization was all about. I found a small office in a strip mall, and four people. Is this group really trying to solve the global water crisis? My biggest concern was, 'Can I make a real difference? Is this worth moving my family to North

Carolina for?' I spent time learning more about the organization and its incredible work, but it wasn't until I went to Haiti and visited a local office that I got my answer. A little boy walked in with his mother. The boy looked like he was three years old. The interpreter told me he was actually six, but he had suffered from diarrhea his entire childhood because of the lack of clean water. Due to his sickness, his inability to maintain any nutrients had prevented him from growing. This totally rocked me. I realized there was little I could do for the billions of people who lack access to clean water, but, for that kid, that day, we could solve this problem by providing a simple water filter that would change his life. And tomorrow, we could do the same for the next kid, and the next. That was worth moving for."

"Climbing the corporate ladder, and moving up and to the right, is seemingly the right thing to do."

"At Wine To Water, I saw another team, small but bold enough to take on this ambitious mission of providing people clean water all around the world. Even though the mission seemed overwhelming, I was confident I could help them grow and expand their impact, as I had on my previous teams. Many others, even those close to me, expected me to take on a new tech job with a multi-billion dollar company in New York. On paper, that made sense. Climbing the corporate ladder, and moving up and to the right, is seemingly the right thing to do. But my wife and I decided to wipe the slate clean-it was time to create our own path. This decision has opened our eyes. There's so much more possible when we take a chance to be something bigger than ourselves or our own ambitions.

Returns that are real

"And now, my journey has taken its next step. Inspired by the great work I witnessed at Wine To Water for over five years, I'm on a new mission to help connect hard-earned capital from people and companies to life-altering change initiatives."

"When you contribute, the rewards are ten times higher."

Nicholas F. Horney, Ph.D. 143

Since 2014, David's mind has shifted from a small box of expectations to anything is possible. "We need to open ourselves up to that possibility. In this world, it is easy to think about what I can accumulate. But, over and over, I know being my best self demands that I consider first what I can contribute, how I can bring my talents to the table to help build better companies and society. Those returns are real. When you contribute, the rewards are ten times higher, and, I believe, even financially. If you're contributing to making things better in a sincere and authentic way, people want to be involved and want to contribute.

"I am compelled to help companies think about this and what it might mean for them. I am convinced, and I think the data supports this, that a company can improve its health and even its financial performance by being an honest and responsible citizen organization of the world. But all too often, it seems we're afraid to get in those waters. It takes leadership to dive in first. I want to invite others to be that leader, dive into those dark waters, and find their deeper purpose. Even if that sounds frightening."

"If we focus on purpose and strip away noise and false responsibilities, we will see with clarity who we're supposed to be. I'm here to help others reach their full potential. I share my story, experiences, and gifts in order to maximize my impact on the world and empower others to do the same."

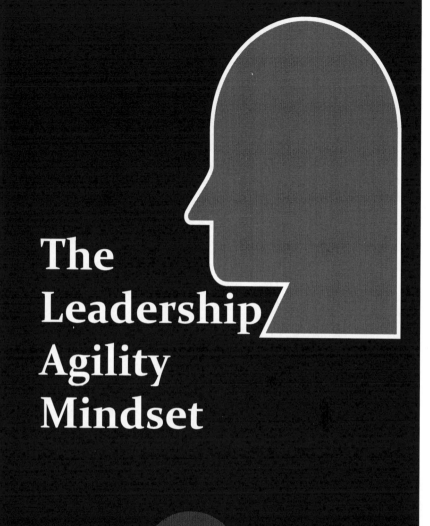

The
Leadership
Agility
Mindset

Leadership Agility Mindset

Mindset -- A way of thinking; an attitude or opinion, especially a habitual one.

Mindset can be summarized as your "frame of mind" which is used to help guide behavior. The good news is that you can develop and strengthen your mindset. Athletic coaches are often puzzled when they look back over their careers and realize that some of their most talented athletes—athletes who seemed to have everything-- never achieved success. Why? The same is true of Leadership and Agile coaches who are frustrated that leaders never seem to fully embrace the characteristics necessary to demonstrate leadership agility. The answer is that Leaders just like athletes didn't have the right mindset.

Adm. John Richardson: "In some cases, leaders may have to start with an admission to themselves and to their teams: we got started on a bad set of assumptions. We may have thought that this was going to be a relatively temporary departure and that we would just kind of toughen up, survive this thing, and then go back to normal. And what we're finding is that it wasn't as temporary as we thought; it's more of a departure than we anticipated. Leaders may have to move to a mindset that's focused not only on landing at a new normal, but also toward a mindset that recognizes that this is where we are for the foreseeable future. It's hard to predict when conditions will change, and so success depends on managing the energy we have and conserving it for the long haul. The stakes are really high, and when the stakes are high, many leaders naturally tend to feel they have to be there all the time, to make all the decisions. But if you can't conserve your energy, you're in trouble. That's when you start making big mistakes." (McKinsey & Company, "Reenergizing an exhausted organization: A conversation with Admiral John Richardson," December 2020).

Nicholas F. Horney, Ph.D.   149

As you will discover in the chapter on Leadership Agility Personality, research has revealed that personality can be defined as a state or trait. A mindset of Leadership Agility could also be characterized as a state or trait. As a **trait,** the Leadership Agility Mindset would reflect a more enduring characteristic and predictive of Leadership Agility Fitness behaviors. On the other hand, if the Leadership Agility Mindset is a **state,** it might reflect situational Leadership Agility behavior depending upon the situation at hand.

Our mindset rarely creates problems when we are alone. On our own, we can view the world through our unique perceptual filter and assume our thoughts are correct and more-or-less shared by others. However, the addition of one or more people introduces complexity because our mindset is now confronted by the differing ideas and views of another human. We know these differences are expected. We must learn to navigate a variety of mindsets to maximize the insights we use when we make decisions and create output at work, and in life.

"Mindset has moved up, from 4th in 2019 and 6th in 2018, to be the **second-highest top of mind challenge to business agility.** Respondents report that many traditional business models, designed around control, predictability, a skill-based exchangeable workforce, and formalized activities, are still prevalent in their organizations. In addition, these industrial age practices form the basis of their work culture. Whereas, for organizations with high business agility maturity, an agile mindset is the cornerstone of their culture. Agile mindset is usually associated with a growth mindset, market experimentation, psychological safety, and continuous delivery of value." (BAI, Business Agility Report, 2020) BAI recommends "Provide coaching and mentoring on the agile mindset to all levels of the organization, including leaders, workers, and every role in between. Because we are talking about a mindset shift, and not just learning a new process or tool, your people will need more than just classroom training. Invest in professional coaches who strive for mastery in business agility and build internal competencies so that you can provide ongoing coaching as part of your organization's pursuit of continuous improvement." (BAI, The Business Agility Report: Responding to Disruption, 3rd Edition, 2020)

US Navy Special Operations – Applying an Agility Mindset

I served as a Navy Special Operations Officer (retired Captain) for 23 years (Active Duty and Reserves). Most recently, the past five years I have provided coaching support for a non-profit organizations involved with successful transition of Navy SEALs to the civilian world of work. The Honor Foundation, specializes in executive education (100 hours), career coaching and professional development to prepare Special Operations personnel for transition to a non-military career.

SEAL training may seem quite different than any planning or preparation business leaders take on. But these days, in a VUCA (Volatile, Uncertain, Complex and Ambiguous) world, understanding how to anticipate problems, act quickly when the unexpected occurs and execute confidently in ambiguous situations is invaluable. Navy SEALs understand how to operate in this landscape of pandemonium.

Navy SEALs train relentlessly to perform at the highest levels in rapidly changing environments. Their lives and their mission depend upon it. In business, the life of the enterprise and the tenure of its leadership may depend on performing confidently in high-stress though hopefully not life-threatening situations. Navy SEALs have the ability to be at their absolute best while handling the worst possible situations. This is because they demonstrate both a leadership agility mindset and associated behavior to persevere at a high level in a team environment.

The Context of a Navy SEAL

Forget what you have seen in the movies about Navy SEALs. The real-life Navy SEAL training and experience is even more challenging than what you may see on the big screen. Often heading out to parts unknown at a moment's notice on a secret mission, their bags are always packed and ready to travel. As a SEAL hugs his wife and kids, he is unable to share any information about his mission -- where he will be and when he will return. Members of SEAL Teams are expected to honor a code of silence about their missions. This is the true essence of an elite performer working in a VUCA (volatile, uncertain, complex and ambiguous) environment. It is as much of a mental challenge as a physical one.

Nicholas F. Horney, Ph.D.   151

Now imagine a career SEAL with over 20 years of experience, sitting in his new office, weeks after his retirement, looking at a company's strategic plan and having no idea what some of terminology on the plan means (e.g., EBITDA, market share, product brand, gig economy, etc.). There are no resources being presented and no intelligence reports coming to him. He doesn't know what words to use to search in Google, and there is no mentor to help him understand this information and how it applies to his new company. For most of his career, the focus has been on "the team" and not himself as an individual. He has managed a $100 million dollar budget to purchase SEAL Team equipment and successfully achieved objectives of covert operations against the war on terror. He's concerned about making payroll after hiring two of his SEAL teammates and stresses about ensuring their financial security. After serving as an effective leader in a high-performing team environment, this situation represents a significant change and new challenge for a SEAL.

The Navy SEALs — the acronym stands for Sea, Air, Land forces — evolved from the frogmen of World War II. They are often deployed on missions which may involve terrorist threats. For example, in 2009, SEALs jumped out of cargo planes into the Indian Ocean with their specially designed assault boats to rescue the captain of the Maersk Alabama, a container ship hijacked by Somali pirates. The SEALs parachuted with swim fins strapped over their boots after releasing four boats — small, fast and equipped with stealth features to evade radar — that were each suspended by a canopy of multiple parachutes. SEAL snipers eventually killed three of the pirates.

To prepare for the SEAL deployments on these VUCA missions, each team member will have successfully completed six months of long torturous runs in the soft sand, midnight swims in the cold water off San Diego, obstacles courses, unending calisthenics, days without sleep and always being cold, wet and miserable. At least twice a week, the trainees were required to run the obstacle course. The obstacle course contained 25 obstacles including a 10-foot high wall, a 30-foot cargo net and a barbed wire crawl, to name a few. But the most challenging obstacle was the slide for life. It had a three-level 30-foot tower at one end and a one-level tower at the other. In between was a 200 foot-long rope. Each SEAL prospect climbs the three-tiered tower and once at the top, grabs the rope, swings underneath the rope and pulls himself hand-over-hand until at the other end. The ninth week of training is referred to as "Hell Week." It is six days of no sleep, constant physical and mental harassment, and one special day at the Mud Flats. The Mud Flats is an area located between San Diego and Tijuana where the water runs off and creates the Tijuana slues, a swampy patch of terrain where the mud will engulf you.

The 6-month training is completed while being constantly harassed by professionally-trained instructors who seek to find those participants weak of mind and body and eliminate them from ever becoming a Navy SEAL. But, the training also seeks to find those who can maintain an agility mindset in an environment of constant stress, chaos, failure and hardships. SEAL training could be characterized as a lifetime of challenges crammed into six months.

Each SEAL risks the side effects from blasts from explosions used to breach compounds on raids, repeated assaults and the battering from riding on high-speed assault boats. Some have sustained traumatic brain injuries. SEALs will tell you that in rescues — considered "no-fail" missions — they have to move faster and expose themselves to greater risk than on any other type of operation so that they can protect hostages from being harmed.

The heavy emphasis by the Navy SEALs on team versus individual success creates one of the biggest challenges for an executive coach. Each individual SEAL will stress team results versus individual contributions to mission success. While on active duty as a SEAL, each person will have no personal identification on LinkedIn, Facebook or any other social media. In addition, the secrecy of the SEAL missions limits the number and diversity of specific examples to illustrate competencies demonstrated by a SEAL which can be beneficial to coaching other elite performers.

Profile of Navy SEALs as written by Former Navy SEAL Thomas Hardee

Navy SEALs are screened from early on in training to ensure they possess the focus, mental agility, adaptability, stamina, resilience and poise to efficiently perform in any emergency. Those traits are then honed and reinforced through countless hours of instruction, drills, and scenario-based training to achieve a common result. Special Operators are masters at crisis management.

It is easy to understand why the SEAL Teams invest so heavily in being able to manage a crisis. It is also evident how valuable those skills are to businesses that operate in today's Volatile, Uncertain, Complex and Ambiguous (VUCA) world. A crisis can strike any company anytime, anywhere. The good news is that it is not necessary to possess an elite commando's inherent traits and countless hours of training to employ some of their fundamental techniques. I would like to share five of them:

1. **Plan for contingencies.** A plan in Special Operations always has a section dedicated to contingencies. It is accepted that "no plan survives the first shot." My standard as a senior advisor in the SEALs was always to include contingencies for a minimum of three. What actions to take when the most likely problem occurs. Measures to take when the worst possible problem occurs. And one other hypothetical event that may occur based on an assessment of collective experience and creativity. It is imperative to get the entire team involved in planning contingencies and ensure every stakeholder understands them. The plans that do exist will serve as a framework, to begin with, and adapt as appropriate. The effect can compare to the difference between being buried up to your neck and figuring out how to dig yourself out, or being completely submerged and just struggling to breathe.

2. **Calm is contagious.** If you were to listen to the radio voice conservations of a Special Operations Force, while engaged in combat it may surprise you. The team leaders, the senior advisor, the commander, the Joint Tactical Air Controller, and the supporting aircraft are all discussing status, location, intent, and situation. They understand that everyone is on the net. Those above and those below their position need to see and hear them being in control. That poise ensures everyone that the information transmitted is correct and that the decisions made are informed. Just as calm is contagious, so is panic. The leaders

need to project calm, and the players need to have calm.

3. **Look, listen, communicate, and move.** This is based on a concept for how to react when engaged in battle. It applies to all facets of crisis management. Look with objectivity – understand what is causing the crisis. Listen with compassion – know why the crisis is occurring. Communicate with precision – share what you know, what the intent is, and how we expect to achieve it. And move with conviction – As a group with a shared understanding and common objective.

4. **Know your status.** Who is injured and how bad? How much ammunition do you have left? What is the status of your equipment? These are the first three questions every member of a Special Operations team will need to answer after a crisis. In business, this could be translated to how many projects and efforts have been affected? What resources do we have available? Which processes and programs are still online? The demand is the same. It is vital to know your status. Doing so will allow you to prioritize the effort to re-stabilize the organization and adequately respond to any new crisis that may occur. Sound crisis management is not only about surviving the current issue. It is also about being prepared for the next one.

5. **Debrief.** Discuss what you have learned. What went wrong, when, where, and why? The purpose is not to assign blame. It is about taking ownership of the solutions. It also may be the most difficult to implement. People have a natural tendency to cover up their mistakes, and we all know it when we see it. Acknowledging problems is the key to eliminating them. The Special Operations Community embraces this concept because lives depend on it. Protecting self-interest when lives are on the line is unacceptable. Doing it when profits are on the line is more likely to be tolerated, but it shouldn't be. The leadership must have the awareness and courage to award those who accept accountability and at a minimum, not reward those who dodge it.

When asked to provide a specific example of how he deals with chaotic environments, one SEAL described his tour of duty during the Arab Spring in 2011:

"In Yemen, it was just this constant process of not knowing what's going on in this kind of evolving situation where every day—minute by minute, hour by hour things were changing...We evacuated all non-essential personnel but maintained a small presence [at the Embassy]...You had no idea what was going to happen next....I don't know how to characterize this but I thrive on change. I would prefer to be in an environment that is chaotic or changing or uncertain because I think that it presents an opportunity to do something, to excel, or to respond probably in a place where a lot of people are going to struggle and be frustrated with it."

The following quote from a former Navy SEAL captures the agility mindset required for success.

"People usually think being a SEAL is this intense physical challenge, which there certainly are components of. But most guys who graduate from BUD/S are not physical specimens. I mean, they are above average physically. But all the guys who I went through training with who were the fastest runner, the fastest swimmer, the strongest—all of the really elite athletes—college quarterbacks, Olympic athletes...Those guys usually dropped out fairly early in the program and it wasn't at all because they were physically exhausted or challenged...What I think that points to is more mental characteristics than physical."

As one senior SEAL officer explained, a mindset of agility is developed early in SEALs when they are encouraged to innovate in their training. This philosophy is, paradoxically, reinforced through repeated exposure to failure. The way a SEAL's agility mindset is engrained is through failure. SEALs are allowed to fail, in a controlled environment. You know the old expression: you learn more from your failures than your successes? That's very much part of the culture. You are intended to fail throughout the SEAL training. The focus is on an agility mindset -- can you bounce back from it?

Research – A Navy SEAL's Agility Mindset

McDonald, Norton, and Hodgdon (1990) administered the Hogan Personality Inventory and found that successful SEAL recruits scored higher than drop outs in self-confidence, composure under pressure, amicability, courteousness, and even temperedness. A Gallup study reported that successful SEAL candidates conducted extensive research about the SEAL community such as reading SEAL books and memoirs, watching documentaries and fictional military movies, and conducting internet research. In contrast, unsuccessful SEAL trainees reported that they thought they would give SEAL training 'a try' and came in less physically fit and mentally prepared (Gallup, 2010). Gallup also found that young men who grew up in New England, played water polo, enjoyed chess, and personally knew someone from Special Operation Forces were the most likely candidates to succeed in SEAL training.

Fraher, Branicki and Grint (2016) found that SEALs' develop the agility mindset required to excel on their missions because they possess a high level of comfort with uncertainty and chaos that allows them to innovate and fail as long as they prepared as much as possible, gave their best effort, and learned from the experience. Learning from failure reflects the importance of the SEALs' After Action Review process and implies a willingness to take risks and embrace unconventional thinking (aka – Liberated Thinking). As one senior SEAL officer characterized it, a key SEAL mindset is "the ability to look at a situation and say what can go wrong?" and then build potential solutions while simultaneously recognizing that these plans will likely change (aka – Anticipate Change).

Fraher, Branicki and Grint (2016) also identified new links between individual mindset attributes (*comfort with uncertainty and chaos*) and collective mindset influences (*a positive orientation towards failure*) that combine to co-create a phenomenon that they refer to as "*mindfulness in action.*" According to Fraher, Branicki and Grint (2016), mindfulness in action occurs when High-Reliability Organizations (HROs) achieve an attentive yet flexible focus capable of incorporating multiple realities to assess alternative solutions and take action in dynamic situations. Resulting from Fraher, Branicki and Grint's (2016) research, two broad themes emerged: "comfort with uncertainty and chaos" and a "positive orientation towards failure." (aka – Generate Confidence)

Therefore, a key to a SEAL's ability to accomplish his mission is that he is unencumbered by feelings of trepidation or mental angst that might preclude him from being fully present. SEALs demonstrate a rich awareness of discriminatory detail and a capacity for action by mentally preparing for and acknowledging the wide variety of challenges that they might encounter during the course of their work.

VUCA environments signal SEALs to have an agility mindset, shifting their attention to the immediate present and heightening their sense of alertness for the unanticipated and awareness of multiple, sometimes competing realities. During this shift, the priority becomes achieving only the most immediate goal; one more evolution, one more push-up.

SEALs' intense focus on learning in the present allows them to shrug off failure and move on to the next event. SEALs demonstrated that they can be both attentive to failure yet not become immobilized by the potential repercussions of failing (Fraher, Branicki and Grint, 2016). These developments are able to occur because, as Weick and Sutcliffe note, a reluctance to simplify, sensitivity to operations, commitment to resilience, and a deference to expertise.

Findings in the (Fraher, Branicki and Grint, 2016) study reveal that embedded within SEALs agility mindset is the autonomy to fail and move on, as long as they gave their best effort and learned from the experience. These findings parallel sports psychology studies which report that athletes who can put mistakes behind them report more effective coping skills and greater motivation than those that dwell on failures (Mouratidis & Michou, 2011). SEALs learned though repeated failure during their BUDS training how to adapt to uncertainty and chaos. Fraher, Branicki and Grint (2016) discovered that a SEAL's ability to reconfigure his mistakes into a learning experience ensures that he will not become immobilized by the potential repercussions of failing in the VUCA operating environments of SEAL Teams.

An agility mindset is an important phenomenon to study because a wide range of organizations today must navigate complex, unpredictable environments that pose a significant risk to the organization's survival. An agility mindset provides the guiding principles and proactive leadership mind-set to build collective organizational capabilities for anticipating the evolution of unexpected events and acting resiliently in times of crisis.

One of the most intriguing discoveries of Fraher, Branicki and Grint (2016) study is the fact that some individuals do not just succeed in ambiguous and chaotic contexts but positively thrive in them, seeking out uncomfortable situations that most of us try to avoid. Rather than focusing energy on containing the chaos in these environments, this investigation discovered that SEALs tap into cues which trigger an increase in an agility mindset that fosters creative leadership processes that lead to innovative solutions. In contrast to a presumption that reliability results from stable hierarchical environments in which human operators are controlled through close supervision and rigid procedures, Fraher, Branicki and Grint (2016) discovered a flexible less hierarchical approach improved performance in ambiguous environments by enhancing an agility mindset. Understanding the nature of these dynamics more clearly help the Navy select more suitable candidates for SEAL training and identify success characteristics for career transition by SEALs.

Executive Coaching to Develop an Agility Mindset

Agility Consulting applies a systematic approach to SEAL Coaching gleaned from years of practical experience and ongoing study and research in the areas of coaching, executive development and human behavior. We have found that there are few substitutes for actual hands-on, meaningful organizational experience combined with psychological principals gained from advanced degree programs in psychology when it comes to assisting clients in their development and business challenges. The depth of our expertise coupled with the selective use of assessments reflecting appropriate psychometric rigor enable us to tailor our coaching to each client's unique needs for maximum results in the most cost effective manner possible. We believe our coaching clients and their organizations benefit from pragmatic, laser-focused leadership coaches, not therapists.

Our coaching reflects a *confidential, one-on-one process.* The individual has the opportunity to carefully and openly examine his or her leadership skills and create specific and highly tailored action steps to accomplish development and career goals and organizational objectives.

Effective coaching requires expertise in a wide array of fields including assessment, measurement and evaluation, change management, adult learning and develop-

The AGILE Coach ™ – The OODA Loop Framework

AGILE Coach Process™	OBSERVATION	ORIENTATION	DECISION	ACTION
	Current Situation Assessment	**Gap Analysis** — Current Situation vs. Goals	**Considering Alternatives & Commitment to Change Plan**	**Achieving Personal & Business Results**
	• What are my current personal and professional goals – next 2-3 or 5-10 years? • How do my interests and skills align with my current personal and business goals? • How well does my past performance trends position me for future growth or align with my goals? • How does the personal and business context that I am facing impact me now or in the near term? • How does my leadership behavior and skills contribute to organization success? • How does my view of my leader behavior match-up with my 360° raters – boss, subordinates, peers, etc. • How do I accelerate my development in key competency areas identified to improve performance in my current role or alternative roles?	• What gaps do I have in my leadership portfolio? • What do I need to do to close any important gaps? • How can I map out a development plan to build-on and reinforce my strengths and to improve my developmental needs? • How to best prioritize areas where I need to devote time and attention for improvement gains?	• What actions and feedback will get me to my goals? • What level of commitment is needed by me and/or others to implement the changes? • Am I prepared to make the commitment for the changes needed? • Am I prepared to seek support from my colleagues, my superior and subordinates to help reinforce the changes I am committed to making in my leadership practices?	• Have my personal and business goals been reached? • What impact has been made on what I do and how I do it? • What adjustments do I need to make in my plan? • How have I been tracking, benchmarking and getting on-going feedback relative to the key impact behaviors and results I am trying to improve?
What Happens	**Assessment and Information Gathering**	**Feedback and Planning**	**Commitment to Change**	**Observable Results**
How it Happens	• 360 Degree Interviews • Leadership Agility Profile™ 360 • Agility Personality Profile™ • FIRO – B • Change Style Indicator™ • Hogan Personality Inventory™ • Critical Business Reasoning Inventory™ • Other psychological assessments as appropriate	• Coaching Sessions • Goal Setting • Timeline of Commitments • Leadership Agility Development Guide™ to guide developmental planning	• Real World Assignments • Courses/ Training • Reading/ Research • Shadowing • Role Plays • Video Feedback	• Solicit Feedback • Repeat *LAP 360* • Performance Review • Self Reports • Input from Coach • 3- 6 Month Review • Future Goals
Results	• Self Awareness • Desire to Change • Change Readiness	• Map of Development Needs • Individual Change & Development Plan	• Skill Building • Increased Knowledge • Experience	• Sustained Behavior Change • Accountability • Personal Growth

Feedback Loop

VUCA Masters:
Developing Leadership Agility Fitness for the New World of Work

ment, leadership development, performance management, organizational behavior, and team dynamics. We believe the most effective coaches have an advanced degree in the area of Industrial/Organizational Psychology and encourage any organization considering a coaching program to ask detailed questions about education and experience. The core coaching model (four step coaching process) used by Agility Consulting is referred to as The OODA Loop Framework (based on a framework developed by Korean War fighter pilot Col. John Boyd). Our coaching framework is shown here simply for illustrative purposes.

Our approach to consulting and coaching reflects the VUCA nature of the business world. More specifically, our framework captures the essential ingredients of success as a SEAL. The AGILE Model® represents the agility mindset of Navy SEALs which has been confirmed through interviews with many of the SEALs participating in the training delivered through The Honor Foundation since 2016.

Real-time data enters the sensory awareness of a leader, especially during the challenges presented by a VUCA business environment as well as a SEAL during a mission. These raw, untransformed bits are ubiquitous, without specific form, and do not, at this early stage, provide any substantive decision-specific information. These data enter the decision maker's cognitive sensors as a set of otherwise unpredictable and therefore uncontrollable circumstances and unrecognized, externally generated, "stuff." These are rapid, various, successive, foreign, and potentially threatening to the survival if left unrecognized, unattended, and unresolved. This "rush" of data stresses the ability to make critical decisions unless the decision maker possesses a well-trained or highly intuitive guidance ability to maintain for-the-moment, and a process that can be exploited to create productive survival in the face of otherwise threatening events. An agility mindset creates a well-formed observation ability that integrates and catalogs incoming data at a rapid yet manageable rate, preparing the data for information processing in a coherent prioritized manner. These data include (1) outside information, (2) unfolding circumstances, (3) unfolding interactions with the environment, and (4) components of an implicit guidance control.

While observation provides the data, it is agility mindset that shapes and filters the data into usable decision-sensitive information. This shaping function provides context, urgency or currency, and dimensionality to the phenomena. A SEAL's ability to perform this filtering and prioritization activity flows from the set of interdependent attributes that may be available at any given moment. When faced with a decision situation, the combined effects of genetics, culture, tradition, heritage, expertise, experience, analytical skills, and synthesis engage create the agility mindset.

Understanding how the job requirements will fit the profiles and experience of Navy SEALs is an important context for our coaches to understand in order to reinforce key values that will anchor future behavior development. At the same time, it is also useful for our coaches to be familiar with any internal talent development language, policies, tools and protocols so we can reinforce same set thinking and encourage active use of appropriate development tools.

Agility Mindset Measurement

The Agility Mindset Profile™ is a psychological self-assessment which provides an agility "frame of mind" of a leader in any role or level in the organization. It was created using the framework provided by The Agile Model®.

Agility Mindset Profile

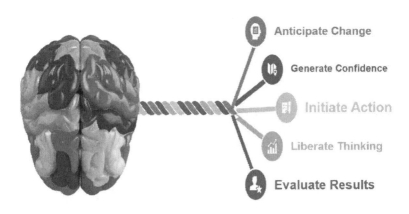

Anticipate Change

Generate Confidence

Initiate Action

Liberate Thinking

Evaluate Results

Albert Einstein Biography

Born in Germany in 1879, Albert Einstein is one of the most celebrated scientists of the Twentieth Century. His theories on relativity laid the framework for a new branch of physics, and Einstein's $E = mc2$ on mass-energy equivalence is one of the most famous formulas in the world. In 1921, he was awarded the Nobel Prize in Physics for his contributions to theoretical development of nuclear physics and encouraging F.D. Roosevelt to start the Manhattan Project, he later spoke out against the use of nuclear weapons.

Born in Germany to Jewish parents, Einstein settled in Switzerland and then, after Hitler's rise to power, the United States. Einstein was a truly global man and one of the undisputed genius' of the Twentieth Century.

Early life Albert Einstein

Einstein was born 14 March 1879, in Ulm the German Empire. His parents were working-class (salesman/engineer) and non-observant Jews. Aged 15, the family moved to Milan, Italy, where his father hoped Albert would become a mechanical engineer. However, despite Einstein's intellect and thirst for knowledge, his early academic reports suggested anything but a glittering career in academia. His teachers found him dim and slow to learn. Part of the problem was that Albert expressed no interest in learning languages and the learning by rote that was popular at the time.

"School failed me, and I failed the school. It bored me. The teachers behaved like Feldwebel (sergeants). I wanted to learn what I wanted to know, but they wanted me to learn for the exam."

At the age of 12, Einstein picked up a book on geometry and read it cover to cover. – He would later refer to it as his 'holy booklet'. He became fascinated by maths and taught himself – becoming acquainted with the great scientific discoveries of the age.

Despite Albert's independent learning, he languished at school. Eventually, he was asked to leave by the authorities because his indifference was setting a bad example to other students.

He applied for admission to the Federal Institute of Technology in Zurich. His first attempt was a failure because he failed exams in botany, zoology and languages. However, he passed the next year and in 1900 became a Swiss citizen.

At college, he met a fellow student Mileva Maric, and after a long friendship, they married in 1903; they had two sons before divorcing several years later.

In 1896 Einstein renounced his German citizenship to avoid military conscription. For five years he was stateless, before successfully applying for Swiss citizenship in 1901. After graduating from Zurich college, he attempted to gain a teaching post but none was forthcoming; instead, he gained a job in the Swiss Patent Office.

While working at the Patent Office, Einstein continued his own scientific discoveries and began radical experiments to consider the nature of light and space.

He published his first scientific paper in 1900, and by 1905 had completed his PhD entitled *"A New Determination of Molecular Dimensions."* In addition to working on his PhD, Einstein also worked feverishly on other papers. In 1905, he published four pivotal scientific works, which would revolutionise modern physics. 1905 would later be referred to as his *'annus mirabilis.'*

Einstein's work started to gain recognition, and he was given a post at the University of Zurich (1909) and, in 1911, was offered the post of full-professor at the Charles-Ferdinand University in Prague (which was then part of Austria-Hungary Empire). He took Austrian-Hungary citizenship to accept the job. In 1914, he returned to Germany and was appointed a director of the Kaiser Wilhelm Institute for Physics. (1914–1932)

Albert Einstein's Scientific Contributions

Quantum Theory

Einstein suggested that light doesn't just travel as waves but as electric currents. This photoelectric effect could force metals to release a tiny stream of particles known as 'quanta'. From this Quantum Theory, other inventors were able to develop devices such as television and movies. He was awarded the Nobel Prize in Physics in 1921.

Special Theory of Relativity

This theory was written in a simple style with no footnotes or academic references. The core of his theory of relativity is that:

"Movement can only be detected and measured as relative movement; the change of position of one body in respect to another."

Thus there is no fixed absolute standard of comparison for judging the motion of the earth or plants. It was revolutionary because previously people had thought time and distance are absolutes. But, Einstein proved this not to be true.

He also said that if electrons travelled at close to the speed of light, their weight would increase.

This lead to Einstein's famous equation:

$E = mc2$

Where E = energy m = mass and c = speed of light.

General Theory of Relativity 1916

Working from a basis of special relativity. Einstein sought to express all physical laws using equations based on mathematical equations.

He devoted the last period of his life trying to formulate a final unified field theory which included a rational explanation for electromagnetism. However, he was to be frustrated in searching for this final breakthrough theory.

Nicholas F. Horney, Ph.D.

Solar eclipse of 1919

In 1911, Einstein predicted the sun's gravity would bend the light of another star. He based this on his new general theory of relativity. On 29 May 1919, during a solar eclipse, British astronomer and physicist Sir Arthur Eddington was able to confirm Einstein's prediction. The news was published in newspapers around the world, and it made Einstein internationally known as a leading physicist. It was also symbolic of international co-operation between British and German scientists after the horrors of the First World War.

In the 1920s, Einstein travelled around the world – including the UK, US, Japan, Palestine and other countries. Einstein gave lectures to packed audiences and became an internationally recognised figure for his work on physics, but also his wider observations on world affairs.

Bohr-Einstein debates

During the 1920s, other scientists started developing the work of Einstein and coming to different conclusions on Quantum Physics. In 1925 and 1926, Einstein took part in debates with Max Born about the nature of relativity and quantum physics. Although the two disagreed on physics, they shared a mutual admiration.

Exile

As a German Jew, Einstein was threatened by the rise of the Nazi party. In 1933, when the Nazi's seized power, they confiscated Einstein's property, and later started burning his books. Einstein, then in England, took an offer to go to Princeton University in the US. He later wrote that he never had strong opinions about race and nationality but saw himself as a citizen of the world.

"I do not believe in race as such. Race is a fraud. All modern people are the conglomeration of so many ethnic mixtures that no pure race remains."

Once in the US, Einstein dedicated himself to a strict discipline of academic study. He would spend no time on maintaining his dress and image. He considered these things 'inessential' and meant less time for his research. Einstein was notoriously absent-minded. In his youth, he once left his suitcase at a friends house. His friend's parents told Einstein's parents: *"That young man will never amount to anything, because he can't remember anything."*

Although a bit of a loner, and happy in his own company, he had a good sense of humour. On January 3, 1943, Einstein received a letter from a girl who was having difficulties with mathematics in her studies. Einstein consoled her when he wrote in reply to her letter

"Do not worry about your difficulties in mathematics. I can assure you that mine are still greater."

Einstein professed belief in a God "Who reveals himself in the harmony of all being". But, he followed no established religion. His view of God sought to establish a harmony between science and religion.

"Science without religion is lame, religion without science is blind."
– Einstein, *Science and Religion (1941)*

Politics of Einstein

Einstein described himself as a Zionist Socialist. He did support the state of Israel but became concerned about the narrow nationalism of the new state. In 1952, he was offered the position as President of Israel, but he declined saying he had:

"neither the natural ability nor the experience to deal with human beings." ... "I am deeply moved by the offer from our State of Israel, and at once saddened and ashamed that I cannot accept it."

Albert Einstein was involved in many civil rights movements such as the American campaign to end lynching. He joined the National Association for the Advancement of Colored People (NAACP) and considered racism, America's worst disease. But he also spoke highly of the meritocracy in American society and the value of being able to speak freely.

Nicholas F. Horney, Ph.D.   **167**

On the outbreak of war in 1939, Einstein wrote to President Roosevelt about the prospect of Germany developing an atomic bomb. He warned Roosevelt that the Germans were working on a bomb with a devastating potential. Roosevelt headed his advice and started the Manhattan project to develop the US atom bomb. But, after the war ended, Einstein reverted to his pacifist views. Einstein said after the war.

"Had I known that the Germans would not succeed in producing an atomic bomb, I would not have lifted a finger." (Newsweek, 10 March 1947)

In the post-war McCarthyite era, Einstein was scrutinised closely for potential Communist links. He wrote an article in favour of socialism, "Why Socialism" (1949) He criticised Capitalism and suggested a democratic socialist alternative. He was also a strong critic of the arms race. Einstein remarked:

"I do not know how the third World War will be fought, but I can tell you what they will use in the Fourth—rocks!"

Einstein was feted as a scientist, but he was a polymath with interests in many fields. In particular, he loved music. He wrote that if he had not been a scientist, he would have been a musician. Einstein played the violin to a high standard.

"I often think in music. I live my daydreams in music. I see my life in terms of music... I get most joy in life out of music."

Einstein died in 1955, at his request his brain and vital organs were removed for scientific study.

Citation: Pettinger, Tejvan. "Biography of Albert Einstein", Oxford, *www.biographyonline.net* 23 Feb. 2008. Updated 2nd March 2017.

References

Allman, W., Fussell, J., & Timmons, M. (2012). High value talent: Identifying, developing, and retaining Naval Special Warfare's best leaders.

Ferguson, P. R. (2012). Targeted recruitment for Naval Special Warfare (SEALs): Connecting NSW to recruit pools with social movement theory. Naval Postgraduate School, Monterey, CA.

Fraher, Amy, Branicki, Layla and Grint, Keith. (2016). Mindfulness in action: discovering how Navy SEALs build capacity for mindfulness in high-reliability organizations. Academy of Management Discoveries.

Gallup. (2010). Psychographic description of successful BUD/S students. Coronado CA: US Navy.

Gebauer, A. (2012). Mindful organizing a paradigm to develop managers. Journal of management education, 37(2), 203-228.

Horney, N.F. (2016). The Gig Economy: A Disruptor Requiring HR Agility. People + Strategy, 39(3), 20-27.

McDonald, D.G., Norton, J.P., Hodgdon, J.A. Training for success in U.S. Navy Special Forces. Aviation Space Environmental Medicine, 1990; 61: 548-54.

Mills, L. J., & Held, J. (2004). Optimizing US Navy SEAL Selection. Paper presented at the 46th Annual International Military Testing Association Conference October.

Mouratidis, A., & Michou, A. (2011). Perfectionism, self-determined motivation, and coping among adolescent athletes. Psychology of Sport and Exercise, 12(4), 355-367.

Nelson, J.K., Zaccaro, S.J., & Herman, J.L. (2010). Strategic Information Provision and Experiential Variety as Tools for Developing Adaptive Leadership Skills, Consulting Psychology Journal: Practice and Research, 62(2), 131-142.

Oswald, F. L., Shaw, A., & Farmer, W. L. (2015). Comparing Simple Scoring With IRT Scoring of Personality Measures: The Navy Computer Adaptive Personality Scales. Applied Psychological Measurement, 39(2), 144-154.

Nicholas F. Horney, Ph.D. 169

Steele, J. (March 5, 2010). *Study points SEAL recruiters toward athletes. San Diego Union Tribune.*

Swierkowski, S. M., & Burrell, R. M. (June 2002). *Tactics, Methods and Techniques to Improve Special Forces In-Service Enlisted Recruiting. (Master of Science in Defense Analysis), Naval Postgraduate School, Monterey, CA.* (http://edocs.nps.edu/npspubs/scholarly/theses/2002/Jun/02Jun_ Swier kowski.pdf)

Vogus, T. J., Rothman, N. B., Sutcliffe, K. M., & Weick, K. E. (2014). *The affective foundations of high-reliability organizing. Journal of Organizational Behavior, 35, 592-596.*

Vogus, T. J., & Welbourne, T. M. (2003). *Structuring for high reliability: HR practices and mindful processes in reliability-seeking organizations. Journal of Organizational Behavior, 24(7), 877-903.*

Weick, K. E., & Sutcliffe, K. M. (2001). *Managing the Unexpected. San Francisco: Jossey-Bass.*

Weick, K. E., & Sutcliffe, K. M. (2006). *Mindfulness and the quality of organizational attention. Organization Science, 17(4), 514-524.*

The Agility Personality

Personality

Psychologists have been studying personality for many years. However, there is little in the Agility literature or research that focuses on the importance of the Agility Personality. As an introduction, personality can be defined as a set of qualities that make a person (or thing) distinct from another. Personality represents a combination of how we see ourselves, how most people see us, and what we need or prefer from others. Our surroundings impact our social expectations—how we perceive and are perceived by others. But what drives the factors that make up these deeply rooted perceptions?

While creating a psychologically safe environment starts with the leader, it takes the cooperation of everyone on a team to succeed. The challenge of aligning the different personalities on your team can seem overwhelming, especially, because of our hidden perceptions. Personality assessments can help leaders embark on this journey.

State and Trait Agility Personality

People often get confused about the difference between a trait and a state. There are clear distinctions in psychology between a state and a trait:

A **trait** is considered to be something that is part of an individual's personality and therefore a long-term characteristic of an individual that shows through their behavior, actions and feelings. It is seen as being a characteristic, feature or quality of an individual. For example, someone who a confident person is stating that this characteristic helps define who they are.

Nicholas F. Horney, Ph.D.   175

A **state** is a temporary condition or characteristic that a person is experiencing for a short period of time. For example, if someone says "I am feeling confident that we can overcome the challenges presented by Covid-19" is describing a more temporary characteristic. States have a limited duration and depend on a person's situation at the time. The difference between climate and weather on a specific day is analogous to the difference between a trait and a state. For example, Wilmington, NC has a warm climate, but on some days it may have cool weather. In the same way, someone who has a trait of confidence may experience a state of anxiety when he or she faces a decision to reduce departmental headcount by 30%.

Agility Personality Research

Many factors are likely to influence a person's tendency to perform well in a VUCA environment. Personality is one of those factors, as it explains to some degree why some individuals have an easy time adapting and adjusting to uncertainty and change, while others struggle (Judge et al., 1999). Indeed, the personal characteristics of a leader can influence not only their own behavior, but also the behaviors of others, thereby influencing organizational success and flexibility (Griffin, Neal, & Parker, 2007; Nadkarni & Herrmann, 2010). To date, however, the personality-related foundations of adaptive performance have not been fully studied.

My firm, Agility Consulting, engaged and worked with an industrial/organizational psychologist, Dr. Ben Baran, to identify the personality-related dimensions of agility through the development of a specific personality assessment. He analyzed more than 150 relevant published studies from top-tier organizational psychology journals. That analysis revealed 10 established constructs that likely relate at the theoretical level with agility: the five factors within the five-factor model of personality, positive and negative affectivity, coping with change, and persistence. He then used an iterative process of building a focused personality assessment. He provided evidence of convergent and divergent validity with these 10 other established constructs along with an established measure of adaptive performance potential.

The Five-Factor Model of Personality, Positive/Negative Affect, and Adaptive Performance The five-factor model (FFM) of personality (Costa & McCrae, 1980) has received significant attention in organizational scholarship and determines in part how an employee performs at work, adjusts to change, and relates to other people. The FFM organized hundreds of trait characteristics into five main personality dimensions: conscientiousness, neuroticism, extraversion, openness to experience, and agreeableness (Costa & McCrae, 1980; McCrae & John, 1992). People who score high on measures of neuroticism (low on measures of emotional stability) are generally described to be unstable, anxious, tense, and insecure. Adjectives associated with extroverted people include energetic, outgoing, assertive, and enthusiastic. People who are imaginative, curious, insightful, and artistic are considered open to experience, and agreeable people are generally kind, trusting, generous, and forgiving. Lastly, conscientiousness describes the extent to which a person is organized, responsible, reliable, and planful (McCrae & John, 1992).

Overall, it appears that emotional stability, openness to experience, and positive affect are highly relevant to adaptive performance. For instance, emotionally stable people and those open to new experiences have been shown to also have a higher level of adaptive task performance (Allworth & Hesketh, 1999). Similarly, both openness to experience and positive affect partially determine whether a person effectively copes with change (Judge et al., 1999).

Leaders who are open to new experiences do not see novel situations as threats. Instead, they are inquisitive—welcoming newness—and may be more willing to take risks (Judge et al., 1999). Therefore, employees who are open to experience should have higher levels of adaptive task performance. Secondly, employees with a positive affect or generally positive outlooks on life have higher confidence, remain calm, have more close personal relationships, and are better able to cope with change (Judge et al., 1999). Lastly, given that emotional stability has been associated with a better ability to cope with stress associated with change, emotionally stable individuals will have an easier time adapting and adjusting despite this change.

Dealing with turbulence in one's work likely requires an ability to cope with change and persist in the face of difficulty. Hardiness, for example, refers to a relatively

Nicholas F. Horney, Ph.D.　177

enduring constellation of personality characteristics that function as a resistance resource as people encounter stressful life events (Kobasa, 1979). Hardy people are more resistant to the negative effects of stress, despite facing considerable set-backs and challenges by having an exceptional coping ability. For instance, research within the military has demonstrated that hardiness is linked to an increased stress tolerance, mental health, and positive coping despite grueling training (Florian, Mikulincer, & Taubman, 1995). Therefore, organizations have begun to recognize that hardy employees may be particularly well suited to positively respond and adapt in an ever-changing work environment (Bartone, Roland, Picano, & Williams, 2008; Callan, 1993).

How people view themselves may influence how they react to change, and such reactions are important regarding the ability to perform in an adaptive manner. Central to this notion is the construct of core self-evaluations, which comprises four facets (Judge, Locke, Durham, & Kluger, 1998): (1) self-efficacy, or the strength of one's faith in one's abilities; (2) self-esteem, or an evaluation of one's worth; (3) locus of control, or the degree to which a person views events as being largely controlled by factors internal or external to him or her; and (4) neuroticism, the facet of the FFM that reflects a lack of emotional stability. People who have a high core self-evaluation should have a higher degree of confidence in their abilities to deal with situations of ambiguity, along with the emotional capacity to cope effectively. Prior research suggests that these characteristics—along with similar ones mentioned above—predict the ability to deal with change (Judge et al., 1999).

Supporting our hypotheses, the agile personality measure correlated positively with adaptive performance potential, positive affect, extraversion, openness, agreeableness, conscientiousness, coping with change, and persistence. Also in alignment with our hypotheses, the agile personality measure correlated negatively with negative affectivity and neuroticism. To further investigate the potential incremental effect of agile personality characteristics on adaptive performance potential, we used hierarchical regression. In the first step, we entered all 10 of the related variables tested in our hypotheses. In the second step, we entered the composite variable for our 36-item agile personality measure (see Table 2). As displayed, the agile personality measure explained an additional 9% of the variance in adaptive performance potential beyond the influence of the 10 other predictors in the model.

VUCA Masters:
Developing Leadership Agility Fitness for the New World of Work

Our data suggest that an agile personality relates strongly with adaptive performance potential. We can report that an evaluation of the five facets of our agility personality measure can be best characterized as having to do with the following five areas: focus (three reverse-scored items, e.g., "I am easily distracted"), confidence (12 items, e.g., "I can succeed in the face of adversity"), proactivity (five items, e.g., "I get things done right away"), optimism (10 items, e.g., "I'm generally positive about where I'm at in life"), and inquisitiveness (six items, e.g., "I love learning about new things"). These subscales also demonstrated high internal consistency, with Cronbach's alpha coefficients as follows: focus (.86), confidence (.91), proactivity (.85), optimism (.85), and inquisitiveness (.83). See the table below for our conceptual definitions of each.

As such, a theoretical implication of this study is that adaptive performance potential appears to have its personality-related foundations in these five aspects. This is an important contribution because it contributes to our knowledge about individual differences between employees and leaders that appear to matter greatly in the increasingly uncertain, fast-paced, and complex world of modern work (Barkema et al., 2002; Horney et al., 2010). At the practical level, we see great potential for increased knowledge about the personality-related foundations of agility. In particular, we see distinct applications in leadership development, because leaders need to know their mindset toward leadership agility as they get ready to take on new roles and responsibilities.

Conceptual Definitions of the Five Facets of Agile Personality

Facet	Definition	Low-Score Description	High-Score Description
Focus	Tends to create goals and concentrate upon them until completion. Stays on track even when it is difficult to do so. Becomes fully engaged in tasks.	Tends to get distracted easily; finds persistence in task or projects difficult to sustain.	Creates clarity of goals and what needs to be done; tends to stay on task until completion; deals well with distractions.
Confidence	Approaches work with a sense of self-assuredness. Has a high degree of trust in own abilities. Eager to face challenges.	Tends to doubt personal capabilities to succeed; gets discouraged easily and often.	Believes in personal capacity to succeed; trusts self from past experience to achieve future goals.
Proactivity	Avoids a reactive mindset. Anticipates tasks and continually looks for ways to make progress. Accepts the need to act without complete information.	Tends to look to others to initiate solutions; less likely to volunteer for new assignments.	Prefers to act versus talk about things; takes action faster and sooner rather than later.
Optimism	Looks for positive aspects of difficult situations. Bounces back after failing to achieve. Finds hidden opportunities within problems or challenges.	Tends to see things in negative light; expects things not to work out more often than not; easily discouraged by failure.	Glass is always mostly full; expects positive outcomes from hard work; encouraging to others; bounces back from failure.
Inquisitiveness	Values the opportunity to learn. Comfortable in new situations. Seeks and benefits from experiences that demand the acquisition of new knowledge or skill.	Prefers low complexity tasks and environments; not comfortable or interested in learning new techniques or technologies.	Displays thirst for discovery and expanding personal knowledge; high curiosity level and willingness to learn.

Note. Definitions, low-score descriptions, and high-score descriptions derived from a conceptual review of items within each of the five factors of agile personality.

See illustration below of a sample page from the Agility Personality Profile report.

Agility Personality Profile™

Low Score Decription	APP™ Score	High Score Description
Tends to get distracted easily; finds persistence in task or projects difficult to sustain	**APP™ Dimension: Focus** — 73 (0 20 40 60 80 100)	Creates clarity of goals and what needs to be done; tends to stay on task until completion; deals well with distractions
Tends to doubt personal capabilities to succeed; gets discouraged easily and often	**APP™ Dimension: Confidence** — 77 (0 20 40 60 80 100)	Believes in personal capacity to succeed; trusts self from past experience to achieve future goals
Tends to look to others to initiate solutions; less likely to volunteer for new assignments	**APP™ Dimension: Proactivity** — 61 (0 20 40 60 80 100)	Prefers to act versus just talk about things; faster and sooner than later
Tends to see things in negative light; expects things not to work out more often than not; easily discouraged by failure	**APP™ Dimension: Optimism** — 63 (0 20 40 60 80 100)	Glass is always mostly full; expects positive outcomes from hard work; encouraging to others; bounces back from failure
Prefers low complexity tasks and environments; not comfortable or interested in learning new techniques or technologies	**APP™ Dimension: Inquisitiveness** — 71 (0 20 40 60 80 100)	Has real thirst for discovery and expanding personal knowledge; high curiosity level and willingness to learn

Nelson Mandela – VUCA Master

Nelson Mandela (1918 – 2013) was a South African political activist who spent over 20 years in prison for his opposition to the apartheid regime; he was released in 1990. In 1994, Mandela was later elected the first leader of a democratic South Africa. He was awarded the Nobel Peace Prize (jointly with F.W. de Klerk) in 1993 for his work in helping to end racial segregation in South Africa. He is considered the father of a democratic South Africa and widely admired for his ability to bring together a nation, previously divided by apartheid. Nelson Mandela is one of the most admired political leaders of the Twentieth and Twenty-First Century for his vision to forgive and forge a new 'rainbow' nation.

"I learned that courage was not the absence of fear, but the triumph over it. The brave man is not he who does not feel afraid, but he who conquers that fear."
– Nelson Mandela

Short Bio of Nelson Mandela

Nelson Mandela was born in Transkei, South Africa on July 18, 1918. He was the son of a local tribal leader of the Tembu tribe. As a youngster, Nelson took part in the activities and initiation ceremonies of his local tribe. However, unlike his father Nelson Mandela gained a full education, studying at the University College of Fort Hare and also the University of Witwatersrand. Nelson was a good student and qualified with a law degree in 1942.

During his time at University, Nelson Mandela became increasingly aware of the racial inequality and injustice faced by non-white people. In 1943, he decided to join the ANC and actively take part in the struggle against apartheid.

As one of the few qualified lawyers, Nelson Mandela was in great demand; also his commitment to the cause saw him promoted through the ranks of the ANC. In 1956, Nelson Mandela, along with several other members of the ANC were arrested and charged with treason. After a lengthy and protracted court case, the defendants were finally acquitted in 1961. However, with the ANC now banned, Nelson Mandela suggested an active armed resistance to the apartheid regime. This led to the formation of Umkhonto we Sizwe, which would act as a guerilla resistance movement. Receiving training in other African countries, the Umkhonto we Sizwe took part in active sabotage.

In 1963, Mandela was again arrested and put on trial for treason. This time the State succeeded in convicting Mandela of plotting to overthrow the government. However, the case received considerable international attention and the apartheid regime of South Africa became under the glare of the international community. At the end of his trial, Nelson Mandela made a long speech, in which he was able to affirm his commitment to the ideals of democracy.

"We believe that South Africa belongs to all the people who live in it, and not to one group, be it black or white. We did not want an interracial war, and tried to avoid it to the last minute."
– Nelson Mandela, Supreme court of South Africa, Pretoria, April 20, 1964

Closing remark at the 1964 trial

"During my lifetime I have dedicated myself to this struggle of the African people. I have fought against white domination, and I have fought against black domination. I have cherished the ideal of a democratic and free society in which all persons live together in harmony and with equal opportunities. It is an ideal which I hope to live for and to achieve. But if needs be, it is an ideal for which I am prepared to die."
Nelson Mandela, Supreme court of South Africa, Pretoria, April 20, 1964. (See: full speech)

Time in Prison

Mandela's death sentence was commuted to life imprisonment and from 1964 –1981 he was incarcerated at Robben Island Prison, off Cape Town. In prison the conditions were sparse; however, Mandela was with many other political prisoners, and there was a strong bond of friendship which helped to make more bearable the difficult prison conditions. Also, in prison, Nelson Mandela was highly disciplined; he would try and study and take part in exercise every day. He later said these year of incarceration in jail were a period of great learning, even if painful. Mandela also created friendships with some of the guards. Mandela would later say that he felt he was fighting the apartheid system and not individual white people. It was in prison that Mandela became aware of the passion that Afrikaners had for rugby, and he developed an interest himself.

During his time in prison, Mandela became increasingly well known throughout the world. Mandela became the best known black leader and was symbolic of the struggle against the apartheid regime. Largely unbeknown to Mandela, his continued imprisonment led to a world-wide pressure for his release. Many countries implemented sanctions on apartheid South Africa. Due to international pressure, from the mid-1980s, the apartheid regime increasingly began to negotiate with the ANC and Nelson Mandela in particular. On many occasions, Mandela was offered a conditional freedom. However, he always refused to put the political ideals of the ANC above his own freedom.

Freedom and a new Rainbow Nation

Eventually, Nelson Mandela was released on February 11, 1990. The day was a huge event for South Africa and the world. His release symbolic of the impending end of apartheid. Following his release there followed protracted negotiations to secure a lasting settlement. The negotiations were tense often against the backdrop of tribal violence. However, in April 1994, South Africa had its first full and fair elections. The ANC, with 65% of the vote, were elected and Nelson Mandela became the first President of the new South Africa.

"The time for the healing of the wounds has come. The moment to bridge the chasms that divide us has come. The time to build is upon us."
Nelson Mandela

As President, he sought to heal the rifts of the past. Despite being mistreated, he was magnanimous in his dealing with his former oppressors. His forgiving and tolerant attitude gained the respect of the whole South African nation and considerably eased the transition to a full democracy.

"If there are dreams about a beautiful South Africa, there are also roads that lead to their goal. Two of these roads could be named goodness and forgiveness."
– Nelson Mandela

In 1995, the Rugby World Cup was held in South Africa. Nelson Mandela was instrumental in encouraging black South Africans to support the 'Springboks' – The Springboks were previously reviled for being a symbol of white supremacy. Mandela surprised many by meeting the Springbok captain, Francois Pienaar, before the World Cup to wish the team well. After an epic final, in which South Africa beat New Zealand, Mandela, wearing a Springbok jersey, presented the trophy to the winning South Africa team. De Klerk later stated Mandela successfully won the hearts of a million white rugby fans.

Nelson Mandela also oversaw the formation of the Truth and Reconciliation Committee in which former crimes of apartheid were investigated, but stressing individual forgiveness and helping the nation to look forward. The Committee was chaired by Desmond Tutu, and Mandela later praised its work.

Nelson Mandela retired from the Presidency in 1999, to be succeeded by Thabo Mbeki. In Mandela's later years, ill health curtailed his public life. However, he did speak out on certain issues. He was very critical of the US-led invasion of Iraq during 2003. Speaking in a Newsweek interview in 2002, he expressed concern at American actions, he said:

"I really wanted to retire and rest and spend more time with my children, my grandchildren and of course with my wife. But the problems are such that for anybody with a conscience who can use whatever influence he may have to try to bring about peace, it's difficult to say no." (10 September 2002)

He has also campaigned to highlight the issue of HIV / AIDS in South Africa.

Mandela was married three times, fathered six children, and had 17 grandchildren. His first wife was Evelyn Ntoko Mase. His second wife was Winnie Madikizela-Mandela, they split after an acrimonious dispute. Winnie was alleged to have an involvement in human rights abuses. Mandela married for a third time on his 80th birthday to Graça Machel.

Nelson Mandela was often referred to as Madiba – his Xhosa clan name.

Nelson Mandela died on 5 December 2013 after a long illness with his family at his side. He was 95.

At his memorial, Barack Obama, the President of the US said:
"We will not likely see the likes of Nelson Mandela ever again, so it falls to us, as best we can, to carry forward the example that he set. He no longer belongs to us; he belongs to the ages."

Citation: Pettinger, Tejvan. "Biography of Nelson Mandela", Oxford, UK. *www.biographyonline.net*. Published: 7th December 2013. Last updated 13th February 2018.

Leadership Team Meeting – Focused on the Agility Personality

Schedule a team meeting (virtual or in person) to discuss the Agility Personality. Ask each person to rate read Nelson Mandela's biography and then rate Mandela's agility personality using the following 5 key characteristics from the Agility Personality Profile (rating scale range ...... 0 = does not demonstrate this behavior to 100 = always exemplifies this behavior which others can follow):

1. **Focus**
Tends to create goals and concentrate upon them until completion. Stays on track even when it's difficult to do so. Becomes fully engaged in tasks.

2. **Confidence**
Approaches work with a sense of self-assuredness. Has a high degree of trust in own abilities. Eager to face challenges.

3. *Proactivity*
Avoids a reactive mindset. Anticipates tasks and continually looks for ways to make progress. Accepts the need to act without complete information.

4. **Optimism**
Looks for positive aspects of difficult situations. Bounces back after failing to achieve. Finds hidden opportunities within problems or challenges.

5. **Inquisitiveness:**
Values the opportunity to learn. Comfortable in new situations. Seeks and benefits from experiences that demand the acquisition of new knowledge or skill.

Have each team member share his/her rating of Mandela's agility personality. As a team, discuss the concept of the Agility Personality and its value in leadership and team effectiveness. To aid in the discussion, I have provided some illustrative samples of low and high scores for the Agility Personality Profile characteristic of FOCUS and CONFIDENCE. To find out more about your Agility Personality, request a copy of the Agility Personality Profile assessment from *http://agilityconsulting.com/*.

Focus: *Tends to create goals and concentrate upon them until completion. Stays on track even when it's difficult to do so. Becomes fully engaged in tasks.*

Limited Tendencies: Tends to get distracted easily; finds persistence in task or projects difficult to sustain	LEVEL 1: APP™ Focus score of 0 to 25
	Development Activities
Exemplar Behaviors	1. Establish an individual time frame (i.e., 24 hours) within which you will accomplish a task. Ask your employees and colleagues to remind you when you have exceeded your targeted time. By setting and adhering to specific time frames you will be developing your ability to act in a timely and decisive fashion.
• Procrastinates to the point of missing deadlines on projects	
• Spends excessive amounts of time on non-task-oriented activities	2. Meet with your manager and make a list of his or her expectations. Use this list to guide your future decisions and actions. By clearly identifying management's expectations you can tailor your actions to assure goal congruence.
• Has great difficulty in making consistent progress on tasks	3. Make a list of all the tasks or projects that you have put off over the last few months. Set yourself a schedule to make decisions on all the issues and keep to it. It is important that you don't let problems or issues linger. By establishing this schedule you will be more likely to focus and act on unresolved issues.
Fair Tendencies: Tends to start projects and tasks with energy, but becomes sidetracked over time	LEVEL 2: APP™ Focus score of 26 to 50
	Development Activities
Exemplar Behaviors	1. Spend some time clarifying the challenges that will be a stretch for you but which you believe you can accomplish. Then pick the one challenge and tackle it, ensuring it's completed prior to starting another.
• Has many more projects started than completed	
• Finds it difficult to say "no" to competing time demands of lesser importance	2. Create and keep a list of your priorities. Discuss these priorities with your manager and others whom depend upon you, revise as necessary, and use this list to guide your daily actions.
• Needs occasional reminders to stay on track	3. Deliberately set time aside during which you will avoid unnecessary interruptions (e.g., social media, surfing the internet, re-checking e-mail) and practice working intently during those time periods.

Good Tendencies: Tends to stick to the task at hand despite distractions; pushes to get the job done	**LEVEL 3: APP™ Focus score of 51 to 75**
	Development Activities
Exemplar Behaviors	1. Identify issues critical to your organizations' success in the future, determine which you might be able to take on and develop expertise in those areas. This exercise will increase your future orientation and help you prioritize upcoming possibilities.
• Meets deadlines on nearly all projects and tasks	
• Consistently delivers high-quality products or services to internal and external customers	2. Examine your customers' needs and identify a particularly promising opportunity. Identify the costs and benefits of acting on this opportunity. Use the results of this analysis to identify the best way to move forward; then, focus yourself and your team on this plan.
• Has a high level of attention to detail	3. Evaluate the systems you currently use to record and document your project work. Use this analysis to establish project performance data. Use these data to set higher standards for new projects in the future.
Excellent Tendencies: Creates clarity of goals and what needs to be done; tends to stay on task until completion; deals well with distractions	**LEVEL 4: APP™ Focus score of 76 to 100**
	Development Activities
Exemplar Behaviors	1. Set aside specific time every week for focusing on the long-term goals of both your organization and your own professional development. Delegate tasks that distract from your ability to focus on the bigger picture.
• Not only gets the job done efficiently, but focuses on doing the most important work first	
• Consistently spends time focusing on long-term important matters instead of daily "firefighting"	2. Maintain knowledge on emerging ideas and changes in the business. Make a list of the opportunities that will result from these changes. Map out, in detail, the steps you need to take in order to capitalize on these opportunities and after thorough analysis make key business decisions.
• Reduces ambiguity for everyone around him or her by demonstrating clarity of purpose	3. Identify a particular risk with tremendous upside potential. Evaluate the issue as extensively as possible. Although all the information may not be available, focus on the key variables and seize the opportunity.

Consequences of Over-Reliance: People who over-rely on their ability to focus can become a bit of a "lone ranger" as opposed to a good team player. They can also fail to remain flexible in the event of changing schedules or demands.

Nicholas F. Horney, Ph.D. 187

Confidence: *Approaches work with a sense of self-assuredness. Has a high degree of trust in own abilities. Eager to face challenges.*

Limited Tendencies: Tends to doubt personal capabilities to succeed; gets discouraged easily and often	LEVEL 1: APP™ Confidence score of 0 to 25
	Development Activities
Exemplar Behaviors	1. Be more persistent when presenting ideas in which you believe. Set a goal to state your opinion or position at least once during a meeting. By practicing this technique you will become more comfortable with presenting ideas.
• Avoids working on tasks outside of one's comfort zone	
• Sticks with familiar boundaries of one's job description	2. Seek regular feedback. On a regular basis, ask others to give you feedback on your performance. Made a note of the positive feedback you receive and use these notes to build your self-image.
• Focuses on past failures as evidence of future potential	3. Identify the situations where you feel least comfortable. Analyze these situations and write down what makes you feel uncomfortable. Then seek a coach to help you identify specific actions to increase your comfort level.
Fair Tendencies: Tends to pursue higher-visibility projects with a great deal of hesitancy; generally stays quiet unless forced to give an opinion	LEVEL 2: APP™ Confidence score of 26 to 50
	Development Activities
Exemplar Behaviors	1. Float ideas. Ask others to listen to an idea you have developed or that has occurred to you and press them to consider the merits. By continually presenting new ideas you will become more comfortable trying innovative approaches.
• Only volunteers ideas in meetings occasionally	
• Typically suggests alternate candidates when offered an opportunity to work on a special project	2. If you find that you back down when you are unsure, commit yourself to studying the issue. Prepare yourself and gather supporting data. Greater preparation will allow you to support your ideas with more confidence.
• Quickly changes a stated opinion when others challenge the idea	3. Visualize a more assertive style. Identify a set of specific behaviors appropriate for yourself that, added together, would constitute a more assertive style. Apply these attributes in situations and evaluate your performance. By practicing these new behaviors you will gain a more complete understanding of your strengths and how to apply them.

VUCA Masters:
Developing Leadership Agility Fitness for the New World of Work

Good Tendencies: Tends to volunteer expertise widely; viewed by others as an assertive team member	LEVEL 3: APP™ Confidence score of 51 to 75
	Development Activities
Exemplar Behaviors • Comfortably states opinions, even if those opinions include unpopular ideas • Sticks up for others and their ideas when appropriate • Uses lessons from challenging experiences in the past to guide actions	1. Adopt a leadership posture. Choose a company goal and demonstrate greater confidence by communicating your strategic and tactical plans for addressing the issue. This type of participation will give you greater exposure to the leadership role and develop your abilities in this area. 2. Look for problem solving situations. Identify problems that affect you but that are not your responsibility and assert yourself by making contributions and coming up with solutions. This will increase your analytic and problem-solving capabilities which will, in turn, increase your willingness to take on even more complex assignments. 3. Before seeking approval for a decision, ask yourself whether it is necessary. If your reason for checking is lack of self-confidence alone, consider implementing the decision without approval. By stretching the limits of your "comfort zone" you will be continually challenging yourself to strengthen areas of weakness.
Excellent Tendencies: Believes in personal capacity to succeed; trusts self from past experience to achieve future goals	LEVEL 4: APP™ Confidence score of 76 to 100
	Development Activities
Exemplar Behaviors • Constructively challenges decisions, strategies or the way things are done in the interest of improvement • Expresses independent views in the face of opposition on issues he/she considers to be critical • Stays courteous and constructive when criticized or provoked	1. Identify policies that do not serve the best interest of your company or your customers. Analyze these policies and develop a plan to change them. Approach your superiors and customers and present your solutions in a diplomatic fashion. By examining and challenging current policies and procedures you will become more confident functioning in areas outside the status quo. 2. When appropriate, question customer complaints. Analyze customer complaints and when you believe that certain complaints are unfounded, explain calmly and clearly that you disagree. This practice should allow you to become more comfortable in questioning customer complaints, where appropriate. 3. Analyze how other functional areas, suppliers or customers interact with your function. Identify individuals who you believe are not acting to promote your joint interests. Meet with these individuals and in a diplomatic fashion raise your concerns and work to achieve a greater partnership. This action will allow you to gain an opportunity to foster better business relations.

Consequences of Over-Reliance: Individuals who are over-reliant on confidence may appear arrogant to their co-workers and superiors. This may alienate these individuals and make it difficult for them to function effectively in their business environment.

Nicholas F. Horney, Ph.D.   189

References

Allworth, E., & Hesketh, B. (1999). Construct-oriented biodata: Capturing change-related and contextually relevant future performance. International Journal of Selection and Assessment, 7(2), 97–111. http://doi.org/10.1111/1468-2389.00110

Barkema, H. G., Baum, J. A. C., & Mannix, E. A. (2002). Management challenges in a new time. Academy of Management Journal, 45(5), 916–930. http://doi.org/10.2307/3069322

Bartone, P. T., Eid, J., Johnsen, B. H., Laberg, J. C., & Snook, S. A. (2009). Big five personality factors, hardiness, and social judgment as predictors of leader performance. Leadership & Organization Development Journal, 30(6), 498–521.

Callan, V. J. (1993). Individual and organizational strategies for coping with organizational change. Work & Stress, 7(1), 63–75. http://doi.org/10.1080/02678379308257050

Costa, P. T., & McCrae, R. R. (1980). Influence of extraversion and neuroticism on subjective well-being: Happy and unhappy people. Journal of Personality and Social Psychology, 38(4), 668–678. http://doi.org/10.1037/0022-3514.38.4.668

Florian, V., Mikulincer, M., & Taubman, O. (1995). Does hardiness contribute to mental health during a stressful real-life situation? The roles of appraisal and coping. Journal of Personality and Social Psychology, 68(4), 687.

Griffin, M. A., Neal, A., & Parker, S. K. (2007). A new model of work role performance: Positive behavior in uncertain and interdependent contexts. Academy of Management Journal, 50(2), 327–347.

Horney, N., Pasmore, B., & O'Shea, T. (2010). Leadership agility: A business imperative for a VUCA world. People & Strategy, 33(4), 32–38.

Judge, T. A., Erez, A., Bono, J. E., & Thoresen, C. J. (2003). The core self-evaluations scale: Development of a measure. Personnel Psychology, 56(2), 303–331. http://doi.org/10.1111/j.1744-6570.2003.tb00152.x15

Judge, T. A., Thoresen, C. J., Pucik, V., & Welbourne, T. M. (1999). Managerial coping with organizational change: A dispositional perspective. Journal of Applied Psychology, 84(1), 107.

Kobasa, S. C. (1979). *Stressful life events, personality, and health: an inquiry into hardiness. Journal of Personality and Social Psychology, 37(1), 1.*

McCrae, R. R., & John, O. P. (1992). *An introduction to the five-factor model and its applications. Journal of Personality, 60(2),* 175–215. *http://doi.org/10.1111/j.1467- 6494.1992.tb00970.x*

Nadkarni, S., & Herrmann, P. O. L. (2010). *CEO personality, strategic flexibility, and firm performance: The case of the Indian business process outsourcing industry. Academy of Management Journal, 53(5),* 1050–1073.

Strategic Leadership Agility

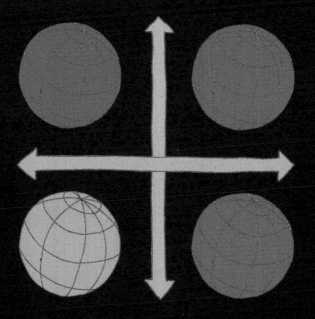

Redefining Talent
For the New World of Work

Stay Ahead of Change with Talent Portfolio Agility™

The following discussion about Talent Portfolio Agility™ is the result of collaborative work during 2017-2020 between Agility Consulting (Dr. Nick Horney) and the Center for Creative Leadership (Dr. George Hallenbeck.)

In 2021, the talent landscape has significantly transformed. While the specifics may vary by industry, no organization was immune to the impact of Covid-19 and other major shifts (e.g., digital disruption) that are already underway. But by applying Leadership Agility Fitness to the New World of Work, you can ride the wave to a more agile and prosperous future instead of being pulled under by the current. Organizations that are able to ride this wave will position themselves to increase engagement with all of their talent, elevate their employer brand, and gain access to a larger talent pool. Additional benefits include reducing vulnerability to shifts in the market by quickly realigning talent strategy, harnessing the diverse and dynamic talent base to accelerate culture change, and thriving during talent shortages.

I am recommending that you approach your leadership agility strategy the way you approach your financial portfolio. When considering strategic financial decisions, the consistent message from financial advisors is to select the right asset based on what are you trying to accomplish, your risk tolerance and unique changes in the market. In a similar way, your strategic leadership agility advisor would recommend managing processes to support all kinds of talent—not just your employees. Much like you would invest in multiple financial assets, you would invest in a diversity of talent. Your strategic talent advisor should encourage you to apply the information regarding the disruptions and their implications to promote talent portfolio readiness and agility.

Nicholas F. Horney, Ph.D.

New World of Work - Everything's Changing

| How the work gets done | When & Where the work gets done | Who does the work | What does the work | Tools for managing talent |

Talent in the New World of Work is changing in five overarching ways and compels organizations to incorporate plans for enterprise-wide leadership agility fitness into their talent strategy:

1. How the Work Gets Done. The work we do on a daily basis is becoming more team-based, project-based, and multi-disciplinary.

2. When and Where the Work Gets Done. Work is increasingly global and virtual, and can happen at any time and any place. We're also seeing a rise in temporary teams, coming together for a specific goal and then dispersing—sometimes referred to as the "Hollywood model" of teamwork.

3. Who Does the Work. Projects are more often staffed with a mix of internal and external talent, and increasingly diverse in age and experience.

4. What Does the Work. Within the next five years, technology could be performing as much as 30% of tasks commonly performed by people in today's workplaces.

5. Tools for Managing the Talent. Big data, predictive analytics, and the rise of talent platforms, such as Seek and Upwork, put powerful tools in the hands of leaders . . . if we know how to use them properly.

These independents are not the "temp" workers of previous decades. They can be found for every level of the organization—from unskilled positions to C-suite roles. The trend has shifted strongly towards individuals pursuing independent careers by choice, not necessity. The search for greater freedom, flexibility, and fulfillment leads some independents to describe their work as more of a calling than a career.

This scenario appeals to an increasingly diverse set of ages and experience levels: Freshly minted graduates by-passing corporate life altogether to establish themselves as solopreneurs, mid-career professionals ready to call their own shots and pursue their passions, and individuals approaching retirement looking to "give something back" with their accumulated wisdom and experience. And it's some of the best, brightest, and highest-paid talent that's trending into this line of work.

Yet, most organizations aren't thinking about how to retain existing employees who are considering independent work, and few are putting any effort into motivating and engaging existing or future freelance workers. Instead, most companies are operating in a decades-old paradigm when it comes to talent. New ways of thinking about—and managing—talent are desperately needed to compete in the digital era. Organizations that can successfully engage and integrate the diverse motivations, skills, and experiences of the growing talent base in the gig economy can tap into more of what it has to offer and gain a talent advantage over their competitors.

If you think about "short-term talent," chances are you think of it as a bandage to address an immediate need. Using independent workers to cover a brief talent gap or when an occasional, specialized skill is required might make sense, but this limited approach can leave a lot on the table. There's much more to be gained by taking a longer-term perspective on short-term talent. This isn't an exhaustive list and only touches on some of the possibilities for tapping into this often underutilized source of talent. We encourage you to further imagine—and experiment with—new approaches to getting the most out of your short-term talent. Here are 5 ways your organization could take a wider view of short-term or independent talent:

1. Experts in Residence. Having a "secret weapon" for strategically important work, or using outside talent to raise a team's collective capabilities, could be a significant asset to your organization.

2. Mentors for Hire. Consider finding someone who could nurture the skills of less experienced employees to prepare them for bigger responsibilities.

3. Brand Ambassadors. Successful freelancers form strong networks with others in their industry and/or profession, and if one of them has a positive experience with your organization, it could help you tap into a whole pool of people who could dramatically enhance your current capabilities. Of course, the opposite effect can also occur.

4. Cultural Catalysts. Finding someone who can bring an innovative mindset or exemplify a particular set of values might help you make an important cultural shift.

5. Transitional Talent. The Rent-a-CXO concept is trending. An independent worker could be the right move if your organization needs to grow rapidly without derailing or needs to weather an unexpected transition. This isn't an exhaustive list and only touches on some of the possibilities for tapping into this often underutilized source of talent. We encourage you to further imagine—and experiment with—new approaches to getting the most out of your short-term talent.

5 Ways Organizations Can Take a Long-Term View of Short-Term Talent

Sure, gig economy workers can fill immediate talent gaps, but there's much to be gained by taking a longer-term perspective. Short-term talent can be:

Experts in Residence	Mentors for Hire	Brand Ambassadors	Cultural Catalysts	Transitional Talent
Freelancers could be your secret weapon for strategic work or supplementing a team's capabilities.	Someone may be able to nurture less experienced employees to prepare them for bigger responsibilities.	Independent contractors often have large networks and can spread the word about your organization.	Bringing in an innovative mindset or a particular set of values might help make important cultural shifts.	Temporary workers could help your organization through rapid growth or unexpected transitions.

The need for new ways of thinking about talent goes beyond the gig economy. To position your organization and its talent for optimal success in a RUPT world, we recommend that you take a strategic approach that we call Talent Portfolio Agility™. Talent Portfolio Agility is defined as the organizational capability and mindset of accomplishing work through a portfolio of talent enabled by strategic leadership agility fitness. This has both a "what" and a "how" component. For the "what" of Talent Portfolio Agility, we suggest thinking about your overall talent equation as part of a three-pronged portfolio, each with two subsets. The first prong is traditional talent— your current full-time and part-time workforce, which likely makes up the bulk of your existing portfolio. The second prong is gig economy talent, including freelance talent locally and globally. And the third—is technology-driven talent, including robotics and artificial intelligence.

The Talent Portfolio

It's important to ensure that your portfolio of leadership agility fitness matches your organization's strategic needs rather than perpetuating what might reflect outmoded leadership profiles out of habit. Just like diversifying your financial portfolio, there are important reasons to diversify and build your talent portfolio so that it reflects a high-level of leadership agility fitness for a New World of Work.

Nicholas F. Horney, Ph.D.   199

Diversify Your Talent Portfolio Like Your Financial Portfolio

FINANCIAL PORTFOLIO

TALENT PORTFOLIO

The New World of Work has been accelerated because of actions taken during the Covid-19 Pandemic. Faced with a variety of factors, including safety, hybrid work design, technology, etc., we're destined for a more complicated and complex future. Many organizations aren't doing enough to pivot. Instead, they're not fully grasping the massive shifts already underway and are functioning in a state of complacency or are paralyzed with inaction ... hoping to a return to the way business was conducted prior to Covid-19. The window of opportunity is closing quickly. That means that VUCA Masters are more critical than ever to figure out the right mix of talent, align the processes or policies to reinforce a Talent Portfolio Agility mindset, and then manage that talent through the lens of strategic leadership agility fitness. By understanding the New World of Work and thinking about how to best attract, engage, and retain your talent, you can take a long-term view of your talent portfolio and break away from old, outdated modes of doing things.

Creating a more agile and adaptive workforce doesn't have to mean a dramatic organizational restructure. It will take time, and will vary by industry, location, organization, and function. But it can be done. Start by exploring some of the questions I've raised in this chapter. Share them with your colleagues, and consider the appropriate near- and long-term approaches that need to be taken. Understand the motivations of current and future independent workers, evaluate how you can work better and more wisely with them in building their leadership agility fitness, and think about how you can integrate a longer-term perspective with multiple types of short-term talent, including technology-driven talent. Demonstrating your Leadership Agility Fitness by focusing on Talent Portfolio Agility might take a while, and the road may be challenging, yet the alternative—sticking your head in the sand—is hardly a prudent proposition. Consider this a tremendous opportunity instead of a potential threat, and you're bound to come out on top.

TPA Audit - Starting Point for your Strategy for Leadership Agility Fitness

The Talent Portfolio Agility Audit™ is a three-step process that examines the gap between TPA best practices and a current state assessment resulting in specific actions to close the gaps.

Step 1: On-line TPA Survey -- The Audit begins with an on-line survey fielded across a broad cross-section of an organization to gain valuable front line perspective on key drivers of TPA.

Step 2: Focused Interviews -- A series of one-on-one interviews exploring best practice categories with carefully selected members from across the organization to developing greater perspective and organizational insight.

Step 3: Summarize Current Talent Management Policies, Communications and Training – Current policies and written practices are summarized.

Step 4: Data Synthesis and Report Preparation – All current talent portfolio data will be synthesized in a report

Step 5: TPA Planning Session -- The finale step in the TPA Audit™ process is a full day planning session with the leadership team where it will:

• Participate in a creative "Strategic TPA Visioning™" exercise

• Identify the demand for a comprehensive TPA strategy from an assessment of the VUCA represented in the organization's environment

Nicholas F. Horney, Ph.D.   201

- Create specific action plans to enhance the organization's Strategy for Leadership Agility Fitness (e.g., Leadership Agility Fitness Profiles, Pre-emptive and Reactive Deployment of Leadership Talent based on their Leadership Agility Fitness Profiles, etc.).

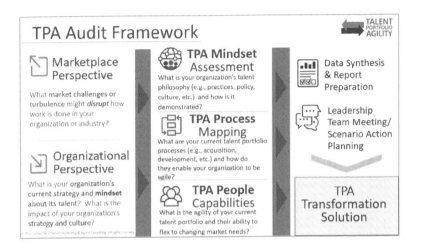

Some typical Talent Portfolio Agility questions to expect for your organization.

Can the 9-Box Talent Review be applied to Free Agents as well as Full-time Employees?

The 9-Box Talent Review has traditionally been a process used by organizations to assess leadership competencies and identify developmental plans for their talent. How can the 9-Box process be applied to the future world of work where talent is represented by a portfolio of full-time employees and free agents?

Research has shown that successful organizations dedicate time and resources to understanding and developing their leadership pipeline (future leaders) and available talent pools (people ready, or in development, for assignments of greater scope or complexity).

The advantages of engaging in robust talent portfolio review process include the following:

Advantages:

- Alignment of the company's future talent needs and the availability of people to meet those needs, whether full-time or free agents;

- A continuous supply of strong candidates who are able to step into key roles along with free agents who can step into interim key assignments;

- Increased opportunities and broader exposure to key areas of the organization, resulting in loyalty and motivation across the workforce;

- Over time, a strong reputation as a great place to work;

- Greater retention of high performer and key contributor full-time employees and free agents.

Pitfalls Avoided

A robust talent portfolio review should be designed to ensure that such common pitfalls as the following are avoided:

- Absence of a talent review of free agents to identify the entire talent portfolio of the workforce demanded by the future world of work;

- Lack of a full-time leadership bench or depth related to key positions or individuals;

- A talent portfolio management plan that is out of date because it has taken too much time to evolve and does not reflect the entire portfolio of talent;

- Individuals who have to wait too long to see any real career movement or key project visibility; potentially resulting in the best full-time talent leaving the company and talented free agents selecting competitor engagements;

- Superficial approaches that result in selection of unqualified or unmotivated individuals for inclusion in development and succession plans.

The Talent Management Review Process Is Designed To:

- Provide the process for a fully integrated leadership development program which identifies development needs for full-time and free agents;

- Foster a systematic, calibrated approach to assessing talent across the organization;

- Build a relationship pipeline that supports a long-term growth by identifying ready-now and future potential talent for succession;

- Continuously upgrade the caliber of talent at all levels of the organization.

What would a 9-Box Talent Portfolio Review look like that focuses on Leadership Agility Fitness?

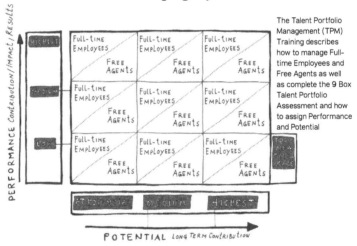

The Talent Portfolio Management (TPM) Training describes how to manage Full-time Employees and Free Agents as well as complete the 9 Box Talent Portfolio Assessment and how to assign Performance and Potential

The 9-Box Talent Portfolio Review could look like the one pictured here. I would evaluate performance and potential of leaders using The Agile Model® to guide current performance as well as potential ratings, whether full-time or free agents. Workers would be assigned to one of the 9 boxes based on their performance (high, medium, low) and potential (high, medium, at potential). Use of the 9-Box drives discussion around the concepts of an individual's performance and potential (to be promoted).

Evaluating Performance and Potential of the Organization's Talent Portfolio

How is performance and potential identified within your organization? One approach is to have a leadership group discuss the types of behaviors and performance required for a full-time employee or free agent to be labeled at a high, medium or low level. Although a formal performance review is not required for most free agents, the talent review process can help clarify those free agents valued as an important component of the organization's talent portfolio. This helps the group set a more external or objective framework against which a person may be evaluated.

In addition, some discussion of how people's performance and potential compares to their peers' may help fine tune placement on the 9-Box Talent Portfolio Review, but a "relative" comparison to peers does not outweigh the comparison against more objective criteria developed by the group.

Underlying Principles of Talent Portfolio Agility

1. The Purpose of Talent Portfolio Review is to Prepare the Organization for the Future World of Work

The Talent Portfolio Review aligns the talent pool with current and future organizational leadership and enterprise needs. The systematic management of this talent portfolio provides the organization with an increased capacity to address current and future organizational challenges.

2. Leadership Capability Can Be Developed

Leadership and the ability to contribute in more complex and challenging roles are attributes that can be developed in individuals. Developing the organization's talent portfolio is a key responsibility of leadership and a systematic process makes focus of talent development more effective.

3. Performance, Potential, and Leadership Characteristics are Central

At the core of TPA is the organizational understanding of an individual's performance, potential, and the degree to which the desired talent characteristics and leadership behaviors are present or can be developed.

Nicholas F. Horney, Ph.D.

4. Candid Dialogue is Critical; Respect for the Individual is Required

Executing a talent portfolio review successfully requires candid discussion about an individual's performance, potential and the existence (or lack) of desired talent characteristics. The absence of real debate leads to the absence of ownership around performance and potential, with the individual being assessed losing a valuable opportunity to receive developmental guidance from their manager.

A quality talent discussion helps align perceptions and appreciates the sensitivity and confidentiality of the assessment process and the development feedback that can follow.

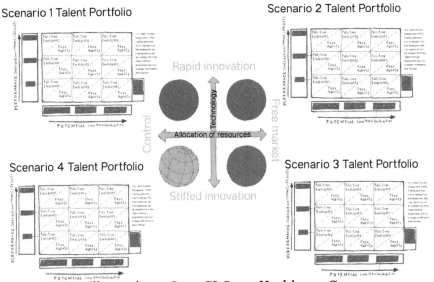

Case Illustration – Sam, CLO at a Healthcare Company

Sam is the Chief Learning Officer of a healthcare company headquartered in Chicago. The number of digital health consumers is growing rapidly in Chicago and her organization isn't currently set up to meet this need. Digital health consumers are using wearables and are looking for healthcare providers that offer apps to integrate with their wearables to streamline and personalize their healthcare solutions. The implications of moving in this direction are huge and the organization hasn't had a good track record in embracing disruptions. If fact, they often struggle to keep up with the market – they must respond faster!

The organization must become the disruptor rather than the disrupted to get a competitive edge. The goal is to be the first with AI that analyzes a patient's data and make recommendations specifically for that individual. At the same time, they need better cybersecurity to protect the information since it would reside on the cloud. Currently, the organization not only doesn't have staff with the right skills to create these new services; they don't even have people with the expertise to create a digital strategy to determine where they need to focus their efforts and optimize how they allocate their resources.

Sam knows this is an issue they need to address quickly. The other large local health care provider has just acquired a HealthTech firm with plans to become the leader in digital health care. The organization simply doesn't have the luxury of time to hire and onboard an entire new department or to reskill members in the IT Department to meet this need. Simply put - a new approach to attracting and retaining premium talent is required.

Solution

Sam shares her concerns with her business development contact at Agility Consulting. Paul sends her a whitepaper about Talent Portfolio Agility (TPA) and a comprehensive RUPT Report for the health care industry. The materials describe how TPA addresses the strategic and tactical challenges her organization is facing stemming from the use of an outdated view of talent management. She is excited by the idea of a more inclusive view of talent including employees, freelancers, AI and believes that freelancers might be a quicker way to bring the required skills and expertise into the organization quickly.

In consultation with Agility Consulting, Sam decides to explore how to transform her organization's approach to talent management including its talent mindset, processes and people. Together, they share with her C-Suite why the organization needs TPA to adapt as quickly as the healthcare industry evolves. They hire Agility Consulting to perform a TPA Briefing to get a sense of where they are and where they need to go.

The TPA Briefing begins with a Discovery Process. Agility Consulting conducts interviews with 12 key senior leaders and surveys 50 employees and freelancers from across the organization. After the data is collected and compiled, Agility Consulting conducts a C-Suite briefing to share the findings and their implications.

Nicholas F. Horney, Ph.D.   207

Outcomes

A TPA analysis identifies gaps in three areas:

1) Mindset (e.g., philosophy, policies, etc.)

2) Processes (e.g., talent strategic planning, acquisition, development, etc.)

3) People (capability to anticipate change, generate confidence, initiate action, liberate thinking and evaluate results)

Addressing these gaps will make the organization more successful as it brings in short-term talent (consultants, IT freelancers, and suppliers) to help create and implement a digital strategy.

With support from senior leadership, Sam leads an initiative to assemble the talent needed to stand up a new Digital Solutions department. The first contractor brought in was a consultant with a great deal of experience creating a digital strategy and determining what skills are required for the new department. This consultant advises the C-suite and the task forces created to explore and implement the new digital strategy. In the process, Sam learns that short-term talent can be used more strategically than filling skills gaps (such as bringing in app developers) or to handle peaks in volume (like on-call nurses).

As a result, the new department is going to contain a combination of short-term and long-term talent. The short-term talent will include digital experts that will create the apps and services required to meet their clients' needs. These outside experts are paired with internal "connectors" who are good at helping understand their clients' needs and sharing new practices throughout the organization. Using this diffusion technique, digital services becomes a core piece of the business intertwined with how service is provided instead of a separate entity.

Throughout the process, Sam learns about how to build TPA capability within her organization and to address talent needs on an ongoing basis as changes happen in the marketplace.

Martin Luther King Biography

Martin Luther King Jr was one of America's most influential civil rights activists. His passionate, but non-violent protests, helped to raise awareness of racial inequalities in America, leading to significant political change. Martin Luther King was also an eloquent orator who captured the imagination and hearts of people, both black and white.

Early Life of Martin Luther King

Martin Luther King, Jr. was born in Atlanta on 15 January 1929. Both his father and grandfather were pastors in an African-American Baptist church. M. Luther King attended Morehouse College in Atlanta, (segregated schooling) and then went to study at Crozer Theological Seminary in Pennsylvania and Boston University. During his time at University Martin Luther King became aware of the vast inequality and injustice faced by black Americans; in particular, he was influenced by Gandhi's philosophy of non-violent protest. The philosophy of Gandhi tied in with the teachings of his Baptist faith. At the age of 24, King married Coretta Scott, a beautiful and talented young woman. After getting married, King became a pastor at Dexter Avenue Baptist Church in Montgomery, Alabama.

Montgomery Bus Boycott

A turning point in the life of Martin Luther King was the Montgomery Bus Boycott which he helped to promote. His boycott also became a turning point in the civil rights struggle – attracting national press for the cause.

It began in innocuous circumstances on 5 December 1955. Rosa Parks, a civil rights activist, refused to give up her seat – she was sitting in a white-only area. This broke the strict segregation of coloured and white people on the Montgomery buses. The bus company refused to back down and so Martin Luther King helped to organise a strike where coloured people refused to use any of the city buses. The boycott lasted for several months, the issue was then brought to the Supreme Court who declared the segregation was unconstitutional.

Civil Rights Movement.

After the success of the Montgomery bus boycott, King and other ministers founded the Southern Christian Leadership Conference (SCLC). This proved to be a nucleus for the growing civil rights movement. Later there would be arguments about the best approach to take. In particular, the 1960s saw the rise of the Black power movement, epitomised by Malcolm X and other black nationalist groups. However, King always remained committed to the ideals of non-violent struggle.

Speeches of Martin Luther King Jr

Martin Luther King was an inspirational and influential speaker; he had the capacity to move and uplift his audiences. In particular, he could offer a vision of hope. He captured the injustice of the time but also felt that this injustice was like a passing cloud. King frequently made references to God, the Bible and his Christian Faith.

"And this is what Jesus means when he said: "How is it that you can see the mote in your brother's eye and not see the beam in your own eye?" Or to put it in Moffatt's translation: "How is it that you see the splinter in your brother's eye and fail to see the plank in your own eye?" And this is one of the tragedies of human nature. So we begin to love our enemies and love those persons that hate us whether in collective life or individual life by looking at ourselves."
– Martin Luther King

His speeches were largely free of revenge, instead focusing on the need to move forward. He was named as Man of the Year by Time magazine in 1963, it followed his famous and iconic *"I Have a Dream Speech"* – delivered in Washington during a civil rights march.

"I have a dream that one day this nation will rise up and live out the true meaning of its creed: "We hold these truths to be self-evident: that all men are created equal." I have a dream that one day on the red hills of Georgia the sons of former slaves and the sons of former slave owners will be able to sit down together at a table of brotherhood"
– Martin Luther King

The following year, Martin Luther King was awarded the Nobel Peace Prize for his work towards social justice. King announced he would turn over the prize money $54,123 to the civil rights movement. With the prestige of the Nobel Prize, King was increasingly consulted by politicians such as Lyndon Johnson.

However, King's opposition to the Vietnam War did not endear him to the Johnson administration; King also began receiving increased scrutiny from the authorities, such as the FBI.

On April 4th, 1968, King was assassinated. It was one day after he had delivered his final speech "I've Been to the Mountaintop"

In his honour, America has instigated a national Martin Luther King Day. He remains symbolic of America's fight for justice and racial equality.

Citation: Pettinger, Tejvan. *"Martin Luther King Biography"*, Oxford, UK. *www.biographyonline.net*, 11th Feb 2008. Last updated 2 March 2018.

Leadership Agility
Fitness
and
Life's Disruptions

Ａs a result of reading this book, you will realize that you do not need to be a US Navy SEAL to be a VUCA Master. How can Leadership Agility Fitness be applied to the way we live our lives? This is the focus of this concluding chapter of this book.

Lori Willis – VUCA Master -- Hereditary cancer and proactive actions she took

Let me introduce you to Lori Willis. I thought it very appropriate to share Lori's personal VUCA Master journey and how her actions demonstrated agility that others can follow. She doesn't think of it as Leadership Agility Fitness, but her actions and public communications about hereditary cancer have created a significant following beyond her family members.

Nicholas F. Horney, Ph.D.

Genetic Testing and Breast Cancer Knowledge really is power when it comes to your health. "I think it was a God thing for sure," says Lori Willis describing how she came to take a genetic test. But it was a test that would change her life—and potentially the lives of those around her. Willis had to reschedule her annual gynecological appointment and this time saw a different doctor. "I was really surprised at how much time she spent looking over my family history," says Willis.

Looking back, Willis shouldn't have been surprised at all. Her grandfather had stomach cancer. Her father had colon cancer. She has what she calls, "... an incredibly strong history of cancer on my dad's side." Flags hadn't gone up in previous visits because there were different types of cancer in the family. Still, her doctor asked her to consider a genetic test.

Willis met Karen Powell, a genetic counselor at Cone Health Cancer Center at Wesley Long Hospital. "Genetic testing is a rapidly growing tool for doctors and patients," says Powell. "Researchers are connecting more and more of the dots between genetic mutations and diseases and conditions. As they do that, we can use genetic testing to help people better understand their risk for developing disease and even guide their treatment." Genetic testing uses blood or saliva, which contains your DNA. DNA is the chemical instructions that make you who you are. Sometimes, those instructions change or mutate. Some of those mutations are meaningful and can cause disease.

"It can get very complicated," says Powell. "Just because you have a mutation doesn't mean you are destined to get a particular illness. It usually only increases your odds of getting a particular illness. So it is very important to have someone who can explain your results, such as a certified genetic counselor, and answer your questions," Powell adds. While Willis admits it was a bit scary, it didn't freak her out when Powell told her she had a mutation in a gene called CHEK2. With her family history, she expected something. CHEK2 mutations are primarily linked to breast cancer and colon cancer. Knowledge is power. "It definitely was. Absolutely," Willis says. And she believes the knowledge saved her life.

Armed with the knowledge of a CHEK2 mutation, doctors asked for a breast MRI, despite nothing showing up on her mammogram and breast ultrasound. And this time they found a very small tumor. A biopsy confirmed cancer. "I never would have had the additional testing if I didn't know about CHEK2," Willis says. "I love that the cancer team looks at your case and comes to you with options," says Willis. Because of her genetic testing and family history of cancer, Willis' medical team at Cone Health Cancer Center recommend a mastectomy.

A woman with a CHEK2 mutation is more likely to develop a second breast cancer than a woman without the mutation. "My mind went straight to 'get them both off'. I went radical because I didn't want to go through this again. The doctors understood," says Willis.

After surgery, Willis is, "Doing great, feeling great and loving life." Willis even appears with her family telling her story on the website of a genetic testing company. She's asked her four brothers, sister and two children to consider genetic testing. Genetic testing is more affordable than it once was. Health insurance may cover genetic testing based on your personal and/or family history of cancer. Willis gets more frequent screening for colon cancer due to her increased risk, but isn't worried. "Knowledge is power," says Willis. "Now I know. I am on top of my health because of genetic testing.

Hurricanes

Create a Plan

Ready.gov has a wealth of information available on preparedness for any disaster. You should become familiar with the guidelines and suggestions for disasters specific to your area, then make a plan for your family.

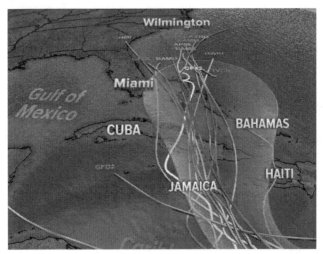

A disaster plan should include the following components:

• **Designate an out-of-town contact person.** Choose a friend or relative who lives out of town to be a contact person. Let this person know that you will contact them to let them know your status and location after a disaster and make sure every family member has this person's phone number. Consider giving the contact person information such as insurance policy numbers and copies of important papers.

• **Choose a Meeting Location.** There should be an established meeting location that every family member knows, should you get separated by a disaster.

• **Make a Communication Plan.** Give important phone numbers to each family member so everyone can contact each other and designated contacts after a disaster. This should be a physical written or printed list, in case phone batteries die and charging is not possible. Make sure children know how and when to make emergency phone calls.

- **Designate Escape Routes.** Make sure everyone knows escape plans for every possible disaster. For example, create several escape routes in case of fire, separate instructions for tornados, etc.

- **Make a Floor Plan.** Create a floor plan of every level of a home that includes windows, doors, stairways, large furniture, disaster supplies, fire extinguishers, utility shut-off points, collapsible ladders, and any other relevant information.

- **Make an Alternative Plan for Special Needs.** For family members with special needs, make a plan to ensure that these people have necessary assistance.

- **Plan for Pets.** Make a plan to evacuate with pets, if necessary. Most emergency shelters don't allow pets, so make sure you know which ones do and make a plan for where you will go. Ready.gov has many resources for evacuating with pets.

Stay Informed

It's time to embrace your inner prepping nerd and become more informed about disasters and emergencies likely to occur where you live. This is even more important if you're a parent or in a leadership role because you'll likely have others depending on you to make decisions. Reading articles like this is a great place to start. Knowledge is half of preparedness.

1. **Learn about how to receive emergency alerts and warnings.** Cell phone providers, broadcasting and streaming services, and NOAA all send them out. While access to the weather on TV, identify likely scenarios for the route of the hurricane.

2. **Research likely disasters where you live:** Know ahead of time how to handle hurricanes, tornados, blizzards, whatever is likely to occur in your area. Make sure you stay informed about local community response plans, emergency shelters, and evacuation plans.

3. **Learn how to maintain your kit.** Revisit your kits yearly to assess changing needs. Some supplies expire, so it's important to check and replenish as needed every six months. For more details, read REI's <u>How to Maintain Your Emergency Kit.</u>

Nicholas F. Horney, Ph.D. 219

Basic items

If this remains as a list only, with no action, you have only demonstrated the Anticipate Change portion of Leadership Agility Fitness. By preparing the items on the list and discussing how the items on the list will be used in case of a hurricane with your family and friends, then you have demonstrated the other key elements of Leadership Agility Fitness. You have Generated Confidence and Initiated Action by sharing the list, engaging your family in discussion about hurricane scenarios, and partnered with your family in preparation planning and execution. The additional step of practicing what you would do as a family in case of a hurricane along with a feedback session to talk through how the "test" went and ask for feedback and modify plans accordingly.

Food/Water/Heat

- Case of bottled water
- Water containers (sturdy, wide-mouthed bottle preferred)
- Water treatment supplies (1 gallon per person per day)
- Dehydrated food & energy bars; canned food (and can opener)
- Pots and pans, plates and cups and utensils
- Camping stove and fuel Lighter
- Long stick matches
- Tea candles
- Fill trash cans with water
- Fill bathtub with water
- Fire extinguisher

Tools & Shelter

- Have tool available to shut off water supply in yard

- Large multi-tool; wrench or pliers (to turn off utilities)
- Dust mask (to filter contaminated air)
- Plastic sheeting/tarp (to shelter-in-place)
- Work gloves
- Duct tape
- 1 sleeping bag or warm blanket per person
- Change of clothing
- Sturdy, comfortable walking shoes

- Warm clothing layers
- Rain jacket and pants

Hurricane Kit Storage

- Plastic tub for a home kit
- Backpack for a personal kit

(Everyone should know where they are located)

First Aid & Sanitation

Well stocked First Aid Kit and supplies are essential. Common items like band-aids and Neosporin are essential, but most first aid kits don't include life-saving items like tourniquets and chest seals.

- Prescription meds and medical items (like glasses or contacts)
- Common ailment OTC meds (Benadryl, Ibuprofen, GI meds, etc.)
- Moist towelettes, hand sanitizer, garbage bags and menstrual products
- Toilet paper
- Towels
- Household liquid bleach -> (no colors or additives) for disinfecting (1 part bleach/9 parts water) or water treatment (16 drops in 1 gallon of water)
- Honey

Communications & Lights

- Headlamp or flashlight
- Whistle to signal for help
- Battery-powered or hand- crank radio (for news and weather alerts)
- Cell phones and chargers
- Two-way radios (for short-range, phone-free communication)
- Extra batteries for all electronics
- External electronics charger
- Small mirror
- Glow sticks

Evacuation & Key Documents

- Extra set of home and car keys
- Cash (in small bills because businesses might not be able to make change)
- Local maps
- A laminated copy of your emergency plan

Nicholas F. Horney, Ph.D. 221

- Laminated copy of equipment checklist
- Laminated copy of emergency numbers, friends, family "calling tree"
- Copies of important documents (Rx list, medical history, deed/lease to home, passports, birth certificates, insurance policies, etc.)

Kids, Pets & Entertainment

- Infant formula and bottles, diapers
- Pet food, ID, meds & supplies; extra water for your pet
- Paper and pencil and Sharpie
- Books, games, puzzles, deck of cards

Miscellaneous

- Gas/fuel
- Generator
- Solar Charger
- Compass

Whether you are confronting significant health challenges as Lori Willis was or living in an area where the likelihood of a hurricane is relatively high, the application of leadership agility fitness is as relevant to life and well-being as in a work situation. What VUCA challenge will you be facing in the future? I have provided some recommended techniques below to engage others in preparing for future VUCA challenges.

Creativity Techniques to Prepare for VUCA in Work and Life

Engage with your significant others or members of your team when faced with future VUCA challenges. Try some of the following creativity techniques (liberate thinking) to help you generate confidence from others through anticipating change from future VUCA challenges, taking action and evaluating the results of those actions.

Play the Critic
Context: For each solution to the challenge, develop as many objections and criticisms as possible. Then overcome the objections with new solutions to the challenge.

Action: Start with a list of potential solutions to the challenge. Then divide the team into smaller groups of two or three and ask each "mini-team" to look for weak areas in the solutions. Identify any areas where you aren't 100% certain about the solutions and chart all potential issues. Then come together as a group and share the critiques, building on current solutions and crating new ones.

Reaction: What can you learn from playing the critic? How did the critiques lead to better, stronger solutions? How does this make you think differently about your process for approaching challenges?

Why and Why Not?
Context: Ask "why" and "why not" to force yourself and your team to explore and challenge your assumptions.

Action: Each person on the team spends a few minutes listing thoughts they believe to be true about their challenge. This could range from assumptions, perceived obstacles, goals, etc. Then together review the lists, posting them on a flip chart, and tor each thought ask either "why" or "why not" to challenge perceptions and see new possibilities for ways to think about the challenge.

Reaction: Why do you hold certain things to be true? How does using "why" – type questions change your original assumptions about the challenge? How does going deeper into underlying assumptions help you look at potential solutions differently?

Nicholas F. Horney, Ph.D.   223

Another Company

Context: Look at your challenge from the viewpoint of another company and try to solve it from their unique perspective.

Action: Using your challenge, ask each team member to approach the challenge from another brand's perspective. Choose any brand that you know and love. How would Google solve it? How would Singapore Airlines do it? How would Nike approach it? After each team member has developed their solutions based on thinking from another brand's point of view, come together to share the ideas. Than as a group, continue to build on the ideas, role-playing as if you are an internal team at another company.

Reaction: Did the role-playing exercise get you out of your typical modes of thinking? In what ways? Did taking on characteristics of other brands inspire you to be more daring? More creative? More strategic? More AGILE?

View from the Past

Context: Often, different challenges can call for very similar solutions. Leverage the solutions you have created for similar challenges as you work on your current challenge.

Action: First, ask each individual on your team to list their ideas for past challenges that have some commonalities with the current challenge you are trying to solve. Second, have each person share their ideas with the team, making sure they explain how they think the challenges are similar. Next, discuss how you can shift, adjust, and be inspired by each idea to relate them to your current challenge.

Reaction: Did any of your past ideas solve your current challenge? Were you inspired by your past ideas to create new ideas you might not have otherwise considered?

Brainstorming Questions
Context: Your goal is to develop 50 questions that you feel, if answered well, will help you create new solutions to the challenge you are trying to solve.

Action: Each person on the team spends a few minutes "brainstorming questions" (developing questions) related to the challenge. Then come together as a team and ask each person to share their questions, capturing them on a flip chart. The team will then collaboratively build on each question with even more questions, until there are approximately 50 questions. Remember you are only asking questions – this is not about finding the answers. Next, prioritize the questions by which are the most important to answer and which must be answered first.

Reaction: How did developing and asking these questions change your perspective on the challenge? Did certain questions lead to new insights? Why? Did asking the questions start you thinking about potential solutions?

Day in the Life
Context: Step out of your shoes and into those of your end-user – whether that's a colleague, supplier, partner or consumer – to live in their shoes for a day.

Action: Each member of your group shadows someone from your target/potential target audience to understand the key activities, challenges, and obstacles they face every day. Ask questions along the way and note the moments when they are in need of a solution that you can provide. Then, come back together as a team and discuss each audience's day, developing opportunity spaces for new idea generation.

Reaction: What looks different about where you can interact in the end-user's world now that you have seen it from their point of view? Did you find new opportunities that you wouldn't have thought about if you didn't experience a day in their lives?

Get Inside Their Heads

Context: Don't just talk about or read reports about your customers. Turn to them to help solve your challenge.

Action: Identify at least three internal and/or external customers. Interview each of them to help solve your challenge. Ask for their view of the challenge. Find out what questions they would need answered to help develop ways to solve the challenge. Then brainstorm with them, exploring potential solutions together.

Reaction: Did the customers see the challenge differently than you see it? Does involving your customer in the challenge lead you to stronger ideas, tailored to them?

Form a Panel

Context: Build a panel of your internal or external customers to test your solutions. Share your challenge ideas with them and ask them to collaboratively improve upon the solutions with you.

Action: Invite your customers (include both your fans and those who are tough to please) to be part of a panel that you share ideas with, test products with, and gain insights from. Consider them an extension of your team – by working together to create real-life solutions and ideas that would appeal to customers and fit into their world.

Reaction: What can you learn by having this extended team to work with and help test ideas? Does working with the end-user help you to better understand who you are creating for?

Outside Inspiration

Context: Determine which challenge area you are developing ideas for and explore a variety of different and inspiring stimuli.

Action: Pull together a wide variety of stimuli from the outside (interesting magazines, trend reports, websites, etc.) in spaces other than your own (business, lifestyle, niche, etc.). Each person should choose different stimuli, and as they read through should:

- Think about ways that you can relate what you are reading to your particular challenge

- Write down unique and different insights that can be applied to your challenge

- Based on the insights gained, develop at least three ideas that are related to the challenge

Each person should share their learnings with the team and encourage everyone to build on each other's ideas.

Reaction: How did looking at outside inspiration change your view of the challenge? Were you surprised at how unrelated stimuli can still lead to ideation within an unrelated category? What was the most interesting connection?

Conclusion

As you may recall, I began this book by comparing Leadership Agility Fitness to Physical Fitness as a means to emphasize the importance of regular reflections, based on scientific data, of your Leadership Agility Fitness. I argued for the value of an annual Leadership Agility Fitness exam, whether you rely on an executive coach or not. I provided a tool for you to complete a quick self-assessment of your leadership agility fitness – Leadership Agility Snapshot™.

The world and business environment will continue going through tumultuous changes which requires the discipline to focus on your leadership agility journey through regular check-ups and informed adjustments to your Leadership Agility Fitness Development Plan.

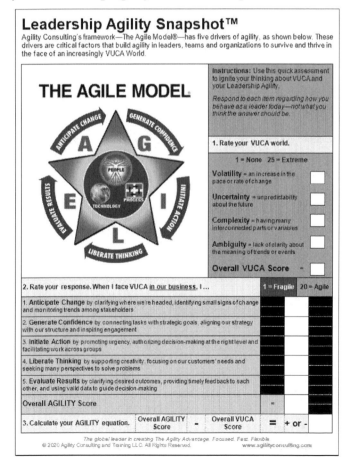

Remember, a **VUCA Master demonstrates strengths in all 5 of the Drivers** reflected in The Agile Model®. Strengths in only one of these Drivers would reflect the following leadership behaviors:

Anticipating Change (Scout) – Strength is in Anticipating Change. This person has exceptional skills at forecasting things around the corner that are not clearly visible or apparent to others. He/she does this through constantly identifying and making sense of trends and patterns. Look to this person to be asking the "what-if" questions and applying scenario thinking.

Generating Confidence (Encourager) – Strength is in Generating Confidence. This is the person who exhibits exceptional self confidence that is demonstrated in ways that are contagious for others. He/she becomes the power source for creating confidence with stakeholders regarding the actions being taken to address change.

Initiating Action (Sprinter) – Strength is in Initiating Action. When something needs to get done, this person has often already begun the task. "Make it happen, time's a wasting or just do it" would be phrases you would often hear from this person.

Liberating Thinking (Liberator) – Strength is in Liberating Thinking. The environment created by this person encourages out-of-the-box thinking. In fact, he/she would ensure that there are opportunities for small tests so that you could fail faster and learn faster from the failure while celebrating the successes.

Evaluating Results (Evaluator) – Strength is in Evaluating Results. This person is metrics-driven and uses a host of resources to measure progress on projects, key initiatives, strategy, etc. You might often hear this person ask, "If you can't measure it, why waste time doing it?"

Start now on your VUCA Master journey by taking the following actions:

1. Complete your baseline Leadership Agility Fitness Exam (e.g., Leadership Agility Profile™ 360 assessment).

2. Work with a Leadership Coach to help prepare your annual Leadership Agility Fitness Development Plan

3. Take action based on your plan

4. Review your plan weekly as you would your physical fitness plan and seek monthly feedback from trusted colleague

5. 12 months later (or when there are significant changes in your role) complete your Leadership Agility Fitness Exam

Nicholas F. Horney, Ph.D.

Nick is a pioneer on the topic of Leadership Agility. His combined experience as an Officer in US Navy Special Operations, Ph.D. Organizational Psychologist, Executive with divisions of Pepsi and Nestle, Change Management Practice Leader at Coopers & Lybrand (predecessor of PWC), Executive Team Member at the Center for Creative Leadership, author of several books on Change Management and Agility, founder of Agility Consulting & Training (2001), equips him to be uniquely qualified to share his insights about developing leadership agility.

Dr. Horney's focus for the past 20 years has been on equipping leaders, teams and organizations to develop and demonstrate agility in a VUCA (volatile, uncertain, complex and ambiguous) environment. In fact, Nick was one of the first to focus on the importance of leadership agility in a VUCA world with his 2010 article – Leadership Agility: A Business Imperative for a VUCA World.

In 2002, The U.S. Patent office awarded Agility Consulting & Training with a **Registered Mark for The AGILE Model®** which is one of the only research-based frameworks for Leadership Agility.

Connect with Nick at
NickHorney@AgilityConsulting.com

Nicholas F. Horney, Ph.D.

Nicholas F. Horney, Ph.D.

VUCA Masters comes in a 2-part set that includes the book and a practitioner's guide for implementing the processes, resources and insights provided in the book. You will appreciate the metaphor of Leadership Agility Fitness since it aligns with the annual health check-up that most of us experience as we identify gaps in our physical fitness and associated plans to enhance our physical fitness. The same is true for our Leadership Agility Fitness and the need to regularly receive our "check-up" through a research-based Leadership Agility assessment with a resulting Leadership Agility development plan focused on improving our Leadership Agility fitness scores.

VUCA Master Profiles -- Examples of individuals profiled in the book as VUCA Masters include some in the past (Martin Luther King, Jr., Amelia Earhart, Mother Teresa, Nelson Mandela and others). In addition, current VUCA Masters profiled include (Matt Stevens – former Commodore with US Navy SEALs, Dr. Koshi Sidney Makai – Psychologist, Bill Gates, Lori Willis – Artist and Hereditary Cancer survivor and others). You will find that these VUCA Masters illustrate how we can demonstrate leadership agility in personal life as well as in business.

You will find VUCA Masters to be an essential resource for the work you do to develop leaders with an agility mindset and associated leadership agility behavior. **Leaders at all levels, Chief Learning Officers, Agile Coaches, Executive Coaches and learning & development professionals will benefit from the VUCA Masters set.**

Available on **a** 📖 ∩ook kobo and in Bookstores near you.

Made in the USA
Columbia, SC
31 January 2022

55019681R00128